# 100 AMAZING FACTS ABOUT AVIATION

2024, Marc Dresgui

# Index

*"Aviation is freedom, in every direction."*

*- Gordon Bennett*

# Introduction

Aviation is much more than just a way to travel. It's a human adventure that defies the laws of nature and gravity. When you open this book, you'll discover a hundred incredible Fact stories that illustrate the daring, ingenuity and pioneering spirit of those who helped make mankind fly. Each Fact is a story, a moment when the impossible became reality.

Whether you're passionate about airplanes or just curious, this book will guide you through historic feats, technological innovations and fascinating anecdotes. You'll learn how aircraft have changed the course of history, how certain inventions have revolutionized the world, and how the quest for the sky has inspired generations of engineers, pilots and dreamers.

Aviation is also a story of courage. From uncertain first flights to daring explorations of our planet's extreme frontiers, every page will remind you that flying has never been an easy task. It's an adventure where every take-off is a victory over fear, every landing a triumph of precision.

As you explore these Facts, you'll encounter iconic figures, extraordinary machines and key moments in aviation history. This journey through time will show you how aviation has evolved, from simple gliders to supersonic aircraft, from solo flights to mass travel.

Take flight with this book and be amazed by the incredible history of aviation. You'll discover a world where the sky is no longer a limit, but a space of endless freedom and exploration. Prepare to be amazed and inspired by these one hundred incredible facts that celebrate the passion of flight.

*Marc Dresqui*

# Fact 1 - The Wright brothers' first flight

December 17, 1903 marks a crucial date in aviation history. On that day, in the windy dunes of Kitty Hawk, North Carolina, brothers Orville and Wilbur Wright successfully flew a heavier-than-air, engine-powered airplane. Their machine, the Flyer, covered 37 meters in 12 seconds at a modest altitude. Although the flight was short, it proved that powered, controlled flight was possible, paving the way for modern aviation.

Orville and Wilbur Wright, originally bicycle manufacturers, used their mechanical expertise to design this revolutionary aircraft. They spent years birdwatching, building gliders and testing various control configurations to ensure that their plane would be stable in flight. The Flyer was equipped with a 12-horsepower gasoline engine and a propeller designed by the brothers themselves. This innovative engine generated the power needed to get the plane off the ground.

The Flyer's first flight was just the beginning of this historic day. The Wright brothers made three more flights that same day, each a little longer than the last. The last flight covered a distance of 260 meters in 59 seconds. Each flight reinforced their conviction that aviation was about to become a reality. Their success soon attracted worldwide attention, although their invention was initially greeted with skepticism by some.

The secret of the Wright brothers' success lay in their methodical, scientific approach to flight. Unlike other inventors of the time, who focused primarily on engine power, the Wrights emphasized aircraft control and stability. They invented a three-axis control system, which enabled the plane to be steered by tilting the wings, orienting the rudder and altering the angle of the ailerons. This system, still used in modern aircraft, was the key to their success.

The Wright brothers' flights marked the beginning of a new era. From that day on, the idea of air travel went from dream to reality. Although aviation's beginnings were modest, the rapid progress that followed led to the aircraft we know today. The Wright brothers' legacy is visible every time a plane takes off, proving that their vision and determination truly changed the world.

# Fact 2 - The fastest plane ever built

The fastest airplane ever built is the North American X-15, an experimental aircraft developed in the 1960s by NASA and the US Air Force. This jewel of technology reached a record speed of Mach 6.7, or around 7,273 km/h, on October 3, 1967, during a flight piloted by William "Pete" Knight. This phenomenal speed made the X-15 not only the fastest aircraft in history, but also a pioneer in research into very high altitude, very high speed flight.

The X-15 was no ordinary aircraft. Designed to explore the limits of hypersonic flight, it was equipped with a specially developed rocket engine, capable of producing immense thrust to propel the aircraft to speeds never before achieved. The aircraft was launched from a B-52 bomber, as it could not take off autonomously. Once released, the X-15 ignited its rocket engine, rapidly climbing to stratospheric altitudes and reaching extreme speeds.

The X-15's design was as revolutionary as its speed. It was built from titanium and inconel alloys, materials capable of withstanding the extreme temperatures generated by air friction at such speeds. Its narrow fuselage, short wings and pointed nose were designed to minimize drag and maximize stability at hypersonic speeds. The data gathered during the X-15 flights were crucial to the future development of supersonic aircraft and space vehicles.

The X-15 was not only fast, it also broke some major technical barriers. It reached altitudes of over 100 kilometers, enabling several pilots to be officially recognized as astronauts. These flights provided valuable information on the effects of high speed and high altitude on aircraft, pilots and instruments, information that contributed directly to U.S. space programs, including the Apollo missions.

Today, the North American X-15 remains unrivalled in aviation speed. It set records that still stand today, and paved the way for numerous technological advances. Its legacy lives on not only in aviation and aerospace, but also in our understanding of high-speed flight. This legendary aircraft continues to inspire engineers and pilots the world over, reminding us that the limits of the possible can always be pushed back.

# Fact 3 - The smallest plane ever to fly

The smallest aircraft ever to take to the skies is the "Starr Bumble Bee II", an engineering marvel that defied the limits of aeronautical miniaturization. Designed and flown by Robert H. Starr in 1988, this aircraft measured just 2.69 meters in length with a wingspan of 1.68 meters. Despite its tiny size, it managed to make successful flights, astonishing the aviation world with its daring performance.

Robert H. Starr, an aviation enthusiast and talented engineer, designed the Bumble Bee II with the aim of breaking the world record for the smallest flyable aircraft. He used lightweight yet robust materials to build a structure capable of withstanding the demands of flight while maintaining extremely reduced dimensions. The specially adapted motor delivered enough power to propel the aircraft safely through the air.

On its maiden flight, the Bumble Bee II demonstrated surprising stability and maneuverability despite its small size. Spectators were amazed to see this miniature airplane take off and gracefully move through the sky. This successful flight enabled Robert H. Starr to realize his dream and inscribe his name in the annals of aviation by setting a new world record.

The design of the Bumble Bee II required meticulous attention to detail and a thorough understanding of aerodynamic principles. Every component was meticulously calibrated to ensure a perfect balance between weight and lift. The flight controls, reduced to the essentials, have been ergonomically arranged to enable the pilot to control the aircraft with precision despite the confined space of the cockpit.

The success of the Bumble Bee II has inspired many engineers and enthusiasts to explore new frontiers in the design of ultra-light, compact aircraft. This remarkable feat illustrates human creativity and ingenuity when it comes to pushing back the boundaries of what is considered possible in aviation. To this day, the Bumble Bee II remains an emblematic symbol of aeronautical innovation and passion for flight.

# Fact 4 - First non-stop transatlantic flight

The first non-stop transatlantic flight is a milestone in aviation history. On June 14, 1919, two British aviators, John Alcock and Arthur Whitten Brown, took off from Newfoundland, Canada, in a modified bomber called the Vickers Vimy. Their daring goal was to cross the North Atlantic to Ireland without a break. After a grueling 16-hour flight, they landed in Clifden, Ireland, on June 15, 1919, completing the first non-stop transatlantic crossing.

Alcock and Brown's flight was not only a technical feat, but also a challenging adventure. During their flight, they had to cope with extreme weather conditions, including thick fog banks and snowstorms. Their plane, the Vickers Vimy, although robust, was not equipped with the modern instruments found in today's aircraft. The aviators had to navigate largely by sight, relying on their expertise and instinct to stay on course over the Atlantic Ocean.

The Vickers Vimy, originally designed as a bomber during the First World War, was specially modified for this crossing. The plane was equipped with two Rolls-Royce engines, each capable of producing 360 horsepower, enabling it to maintain a constant speed during the long flight. Alcock and Brown had to overcome numerous technical difficulties en route, including icing problems and a radio malfunction, which cut them off from all communication with the ground.

Landing in Ireland was a moment of triumph, not only for Alcock and Brown, but for aviation in general. Their success proved that transatlantic flights, once considered impossible, could become a reality. This feat encouraged engineers and pilots the world over to push back the limits of what aircraft could achieve. Alcock and Brown were hailed as heroes and received numerous awards, including the £10,000 prize offered by Britain's Daily Mail newspaper for the first non-stop transatlantic flight.

The legacy of this pioneering flight is immense. Alcock and Brown's crossing paved the way for commercial transatlantic flights, transforming the way continents were connected. Their courage and determination continue to inspire those seeking to push back the frontiers of aviation. This first non-stop transatlantic flight remains one of the most remarkable feats in aviation history, a testament to human ingenuity and the will to overcome the most daunting obstacles.

# Fact 5 - The first solar-powered airplane

The first solar-powered airplane to take to the skies was the Solar Challenger, an innovation that marked a turning point in aviation history. Designed by American engineer Paul MacCready, this revolutionary aircraft made its first flight in 1981. Powered solely by solar energy, it flew an impressive 262 kilometers over the English Channel from Pontoise in France to Manston in England. This flight demonstrated for the first time that solar-powered flight was not only possible, but also capable of covering significant distances.

The Solar Challenger was a lightweight aircraft, built mainly from carbon fiber and Kevlar to minimize weight while maximizing strength. Its wing surface was covered with 16,000 solar cells, which converted sunlight into electrical energy. This energy was stored in batteries and used to power an electric motor, enabling the aircraft to maintain a constant speed of around 65 km/h. The effectiveness of this technology was demonstrated during the Channel crossing, a feat that required meticulous planning and optimum use of the available energy.

The pilot of this historic flight, Stephen Ptacek, played a crucial role in the success of the expedition. He had to navigate through varied weather conditions while carefully managing energy consumption to avoid running out of power mid-flight. The Solar Challenger flew at an altitude of around 3,000 meters, where it benefited from optimal sunlight to maximize the charge of its solar cells. Despite the relatively slow pace of the flight, the technical achievement was immense, symbolizing a major breakthrough in environmentally-friendly aviation.

The idea behind the Solar Challenger grew out of Paul MacCready's earlier success with the Gossamer Albatross, a human-powered aircraft. However, the transition to solar power presented a far more complex challenge. MacCready and his team had to devise innovative solutions to manage the collection, storage and use of solar energy in flight. Their work not only resulted in a world record, but also paved the way for new possibilities in aviation, where sustainability and energy efficiency are becoming priorities.

The flight of the Solar Challenger in 1981 was a dazzling demonstration of the potential of renewable energy in aviation. Since this pioneering flight, many other solar aircraft projects have been inspired by this feat.

# Fact 6 - The world's first jet plane

The world's first jet aircraft, the Heinkel He 178, marked a revolution in aviation history. This German aircraft, designed by engineer Hans von Ohain and built by the Heinkel company, made its maiden flight on August 27, 1939. On that day, the He 178 took off from Marienehe airport, near Rostock, Germany, powered by a jet engine - a completely new technology at the time that was to transform the way aircraft flew.

The Heinkel He 178 was powered by a jet engine designed by von Ohain, one of the pioneers of jet propulsion. Unlike propeller engines, which used the power of an engine to turn a propeller and create lift, the jet engine worked by compressing air, injecting fuel into it, then burning it to produce thrust. This method enabled the aircraft to fly faster and more efficiently at high altitudes, without relying on air density to generate lift, as was the case with propeller engines.

The He 178's design was simple yet innovative, with a light metal structure and monoplane configuration. The jet engine was integrated into the fuselage, a design that was to become the standard for future jet aircraft. Although the He 178 was not intended as a combat aircraft, it served as a crucial prototype for the development of jet technology. It reached a top speed of around 700 km/h during its tests, an impressive speed for its time, demonstrating the enormous potential of jet propulsion.

The He 178's impact on the aviation industry was immediate. This successful flight convinced engineers and military personnel worldwide that the future of aviation lay in jet aircraft. Although the He 178 never went into series production, it paved the way for further developments that soon led to the creation of the first jet fighters, such as the Messerschmitt Me 262, which would enter service a few years later.

Today, the Heinkel He 178 is regarded as a major technological breakthrough. It not only demonstrated that jet propulsion was viable, but also laid the foundations for modern aviation. This first jet aircraft remains an icon of innovation, an example of how a new idea can completely transform a field - in this case, aviation - paving the way for the high-speed aircraft we know today.

# Fact 7 - The airplane that flies backwards

Among the many fascinating feats of aviation, the idea that an airplane can fly backwards seems almost unbelievable. Yet the helicopter, a special type of aircraft, possesses this unique ability. The first to demonstrate this capability was the Sikorsky R-4, a helicopter designed by Igor Sikorsky in the 1940s. Unlike conventional aircraft, the helicopter can not only fly forwards, but also backwards, sideways and even hover, thanks to its rotors, which enable it to generate lift in any direction.

The secret behind this maneuver lies in the design of the helicopter. Instead of using fixed wings like an airplane, a helicopter is equipped with a main rotor, a large propeller placed at the top of the aircraft. By adjusting the angle of the rotor blades, the pilot can control the direction and power of the thrust, enabling the helicopter to move forward or backward. This capability is particularly useful in situations where limited space or obstacles prevent forward flight, such as during rescue operations or surveillance in difficult areas.

The Sikorsky R-4 was the first helicopter to be mass-produced and used by the US armed forces during the Second World War. It proved its worth on missions where the ability to fly backwards was essential. For example, during rescues in hostile environments, where it was crucial to approach a site slowly and be able to quickly reverse course in the event of danger. This unique capability quickly made the helicopter an indispensable tool for the military, rescue services and, later, civilians.

Over the decades, helicopters have evolved to become even more versatile, but the fundamental principle that enables backwards flight has remained the same. Today, modern helicopters like the Apache AH-64 or the Sikorsky UH-60 Black Hawk use advanced rotor systems that not only enable them to fly backwards, but also to perform complex maneuvers with incredible precision. These capabilities make the helicopter one of the most flexible and useful aircraft in aviation.

The helicopter represents a major advance in the history of flight, as it has made it possible to explore aspects of flight that conventional aircraft could not achieve. The ability to fly backwards is just one of the many technical feats that make the helicopter a fascinating aircraft, demonstrating once again human ingenuity in the field of aviation. This type of maneuver continues to capture the imagination, and remains an impressive example of what aeronautical technology can achieve.

# Fact 8 - The largest commercial aircraft

The largest commercial aircraft ever built is the Airbus A380, an air giant that has redefined the standards of commercial aviation. First introduced in 2007, this double-decker aircraft is capable of carrying up to 853 passengers in a densified configuration, although most airlines have opted for more luxurious configurations, accommodating between 500 and 600 passengers. With a wingspan of 79.8 metres and a length of 72.7 metres, the A380 is truly a feat of engineering.

The Airbus A380 was designed to meet the growing demand for air transport on the world's busiest long-haul routes. It has enabled airlines to carry more passengers per flight, reducing the total number of flights required. Its unique full-length double-deck design has maximized available space, while offering passengers unrivalled levels of comfort. More spacious cabins, lounges and even first-class showers have been integrated into certain layouts.

The A380 is not only big, it's also technologically advanced. It is powered by four Rolls-Royce Trent 900 or Engine Alliance GP7200 engines, capable of generating enormous thrust while being more fuel-efficient than previous-generation engines. Thanks to wings specially designed to maximize aerodynamic efficiency, the A380 can fly long distances non-stop, linking cities such as Sydney and Dubai, or London and Singapore, with a maximum range of around 15,000 kilometers.

One of the major challenges in introducing the A380 was adapting it to existing airport infrastructures. Due to its exceptional size, many airports had to make modifications to accommodate this aircraft. Wider runways, adapted boarding bridges and specific maintenance facilities were all necessary to ensure that the A380 could operate safely and efficiently. However, these adjustments have enabled airports to better handle a larger number of passengers with a single aircraft.

Since its introduction, the Airbus A380 has become an aviation icon, symbolizing the pinnacle of luxury, high-capacity air travel. Although the model is no longer in production, it remains an impressive testament to what aerospace engineering can achieve. Each flight of the A380 continues to capture the imagination of aviation enthusiasts and redefine what is possible in the skies.

# Fact 9 - The helicopter that lifts a car

One of the most powerful helicopters ever built is the Mil Mi-26, a veritable colossus of the air. Designed by the Mil design bureau in the Soviet Union, this helicopter is capable of lifting extremely heavy loads, including a car, with disconcerting ease. The Mi-26 made its maiden flight in 1977, and to this day remains the heaviest and most powerful helicopter in production. With an impressive lifting capacity of 20 tonnes, it is used for a wide range of missions, from military transport to disaster relief.

The Mi-26 is equipped with two turbine engines, each producing 11,400 horsepower, enabling it to lift massive loads. To give you an idea, this helicopter could easily lift a medium-sized family car or even an entire bus. It has been used to transport heavy military equipment, armored vehicles, and even for emergency lifting operations, such as during the Chernobyl disaster, where it was used to deposit heavy materials at the site of the damaged reactor.

The size of the Mil Mi-26 is as impressive as its power. It is 40 meters long, with a main rotor 32 meters in diameter. This gigantic rotor is essential for generating the lift needed to carry heavy loads. The helicopter's cabin is also spacious enough to carry vehicles, construction equipment and even troops. Thanks to this versatility, the Mi-26 has been used in humanitarian missions, such as transporting supplies to isolated areas or recovering aircraft in distress from inaccessible places.

The Mi-26's outstanding performance is due not only to its raw power, but also to sophisticated engineering. The flight control system is designed to maintain stability even under maximum loads, and the helicopter is equipped with advanced instrumentation to enable operations in difficult conditions, such as high mountains or polar regions. This helicopter can operate in environments where few other machines could, making it an invaluable asset for the most demanding missions.

The Mil Mi-26 remains a symbol of the power and ingenuity of modern aviation. Its ability to lift objects as heavy as a car or an armored vehicle, while operating in the most extreme conditions, makes it one of the most remarkable helicopters in history. This giant of the skies continues to play a crucial role in complex missions around the world, proving that even the most difficult tasks can be overcome thanks to aeronautical engineering.

# Fact 10 - First airplane marketed as an assembly kit

The idea of being able to build your own airplane at home may sound like something out of a dream, but it's become a reality thanks to the Bowers Fly Baby, the first airplane to be marketed as an assembly kit. Designed by American engineer Peter M. Bowers in the 1960s, the Fly Baby was specially conceived for aviation enthusiasts wishing to create their own aircraft. This simple, lightweight, single-seat wooden monoplane was designed to be assembled in a garage or workshop, enabling enthusiasts to fly an aircraft they had built themselves.

The Bowers Fly Baby concept was born at a time when light aviation was becoming increasingly accessible, but the cost of acquiring an airplane was still prohibitive for many. Peter Bowers designed the aircraft as part of a competition organized by the Experimental Aircraft Association (EAA), aimed at creating a plane that was easy to build and fly. The Fly Baby won the competition in 1962, and its success led to the creation of a kit version, enabling thousands of people to build their own aircraft at relatively low cost.

The Fly Baby kit included detailed plans, a list of materials required and step-by-step instructions to guide the amateur builder through each stage. The main parts, such as spars, ribs and fuselage, were all designed to be made from materials available at local hardware stores. The engine, meanwhile, could be salvaged or purchased separately, adding a customizable dimension to the aircraft. The end result was a lightweight aircraft, capable of taking off and landing over short distances, and offering a safe and enjoyable flying experience.

The Bowers Fly Baby not only enabled aviation enthusiasts to realize their dream of flying in a plane they had built themselves, it also inspired a veritable revolution in amateur aviation. The success of this concept paved the way for other aircraft kits, giving rise to a thriving industry of amateur aircraft construction. Fly Babies continue to fly today, testifying to the durability and popularity of this innovative approach.

The impact of the Bowers Fly Baby goes beyond technical innovation. It democratized access to aviation by offering an affordable alternative to commercial aircraft. Fact's ability to build and fly its own aircraft offered a new form of freedom to aviation enthusiasts, while paying homage to the pioneering spirit of early aviation. The Fly Baby remains an icon of light aviation, representing the ingenuity and determination of those who want to touch the sky with their own hands.

# Fact 11 - The plane that flew around the world

One of the most daring feats in aviation history is undoubtedly the first non-stop, non-refueling circumnavigation of the globe. This feat was accomplished by the Voyager, a light aircraft specially designed for the mission, piloted by Dick Rutan and Jeana Yeager. Voyager took off from Edwards Air Force Base, California, on December 14, 1986, and completed its circumnavigation on December 23 of the same year, having covered 42,000 kilometers in nine days, three minutes and forty-four seconds.

The Voyager was a true feat of engineering, designed by Burt Rutan, Dick Rutan's brother, and famous for his innovations in aviation. The aircraft was built primarily from composite materials, making it both lightweight and robust. With a wingspan of 33.8 meters and an empty weight of just 1,020 kilograms, it carried an impressive 3,180 liters of fuel in tanks occupying most of its fuselage and wings. This design was essential for the long, non-stop flight.

Rutan and Yeager faced many challenges on their journey. The flight traversed a variety of weather conditions, including severe turbulence and storms. Fatigue was a constant enemy, as both pilots had to take turns flying the plane in a very confined space. What's more, the aircraft was so fragile that the slightest turbulence could damage the structure, forcing the pilots to maneuver with extreme caution. Despite these obstacles, their determination and skill enabled them to successfully complete this unprecedented mission.

Voyager's success not only set a new world record, but also demonstrated the incredible advances in the design and construction of ultra-light, energy-efficient aircraft. Rutan and Yeager's feat captivated the world, inspiring many other innovative aviation projects. This non-stop round-the-world flight remains a major milestone in aviation history, underlining the spirit of innovation and perseverance that characterizes great human adventures.

This incredible journey has been celebrated as one of the greatest aeronautical feats of all time. Voyager is now on display at the National Air and Space Museum in Washington, D.C., where it continues to inspire visitors with the story it tells: that of the vision, courage and innovation that enabled an aircraft to circumnavigate the globe without ever stopping, opening up new vistas for the future of aviation.

# Fact 12 - The plane designed to fly into space

The aircraft that was designed to fly into space was the North American X-15, an experimental craft that pushed back the boundaries of aviation and space exploration. Developed in the 1950s by NASA and the US Air Force, the X-15 was a rocket plane capable of flying at suborbital altitudes, reaching the frontiers of space. Between 1959 and 1968, it made 199 flights, several of which enabled its pilots to cross the Kármán line, 100 kilometers above the Earth, considered the limit of space.

The X-15 was powered by a rocket engine that enabled it to reach phenomenal speeds, exceeding Mach 6, or more than 7,200 km/h. This engine used a mixture of hydrogen peroxide and liquid ammonia to generate incredible thrust, capable of propelling the plane to altitudes where the earth's atmosphere becomes extremely tenuous. At these altitudes, the X-15's wings were almost useless, and control of the aircraft depended on small thrusters located on the plane's wings and nose, a system similar to that used by spacecraft.

One of the X-15's most remarkable flights took place on August 22, 1963, when pilot Joseph A. Walker reached an altitude of 107.8 kilometers, becoming one of the first recognized astronauts. This flight demonstrated that the X-15 was capable of navigating the near-space region, opening up new possibilities for manned flight. The aircraft was equipped with sophisticated measuring instruments to gather data on the effects of high altitude and extreme speed on the human body and aircraft structures, providing crucial information for future space missions.

The X-15 was a pioneering aircraft not only for its performance, but also for the innovation it brought to aviation. Its design, with its slim fuselage and short wings, inspired later space shuttle designs. What's more, the experiments carried out on board contributed directly to the development of the Apollo and Space Shuttle programs, the United States' first manned space missions. The X-15 thus served as a bridge between high-speed aviation and space exploration.

Today, the North American X-15 is celebrated as one of the greatest feats of aeronautical engineering. Its daring flights not only pushed back the frontiers of aviation, but also laid the foundations for modern space exploration. This aircraft remains a symbol of daring and innovation, showing what mankind can achieve when it literally aims for the stars.

# Fact 13 - First plane to break the sound barrier

On October 14, 1947, a historic feat was accomplished in the skies over California's Mojave Desert. On that day, US Air Force pilot Chuck Yeager broke the sound barrier for the first time aboard the Bell X-1, a bright orange streamlined aircraft nicknamed "Glamorous Glennis" in honor of his wife. The event marked a turning point in aviation history, demonstrating that the sound barrier, long considered impassable, could be overcome.

The Bell X-1 was designed specifically to explore supersonic speeds. Its aerodynamic design, inspired by a rifle bullet, was crucial in reducing air resistance at extremely high speeds. The aircraft was powered by a liquid-fuel rocket engine capable of generating enough thrust to reach Mach 1, the speed of sound. On his historic flight, Yeager reached a speed of Mach 1.06, or around 1,130 km/h, at an altitude of 13,000 meters, breaking the sound barrier and making history.

The flight was not without risk. At the time, it was thought that breaking the sound barrier would cause turbulence so violent that the plane could break up in mid-air. Yeager himself faced personal challenges: two days before the flight, he had injured himself riding a horse, fracturing two ribs. Fearing he would be removed from the mission, he kept the injury a secret, flying despite the pain. During the flight, the plane shook violently as it approached the speed of sound, but once over the barrier, it became strangely stable, opening up a new era in aviation.

The success of the Bell X-1 and Chuck Yeager not only demonstrated the possibility of supersonic flight, it also spurred engineers to design aircraft capable of flying faster and higher. This first supersonic flight was a catalyst for the development of supersonic fighters and airliners, as well as for aeronautical research in general. It showed that technological limits could be pushed back by human ingenuity and the courage of aviation pioneers.

Today, the Bell X-1 is on display at the National Air and Space Museum in Washington, D.C., as a symbol of an era when the boundaries of speed and flight were constantly re-evaluated. Yeager's flight remains a source of inspiration for pilots and engineers the world over, proving that even the most daunting challenges can be overcome with determination and innovation. This seminal event paved the way for the incredible advances in supersonic aviation we know today.

# Fact 14 - The lightest aircraft ever built

The lightest aircraft ever built is the Stits SA-2A Sky Baby, a true jewel of aeronautical ingenuity. Designed by Ray Stits in 1952, this aircraft weighed in at just 117 kilograms, less than the average weight of a motorcycle. The Sky Baby was conceived with the aim of creating the world's lightest yet most manoeuvrable aircraft, a feat which, despite its tiny size, managed to take to the air and fly stably.

The Sky Baby was barely 3 meters long, with a wingspan of just 2.7 meters. It was powered by an 85-hp Continental C-85 engine, a relatively powerful powerplant for such a small, light aircraft. This light but efficient engine enabled the Sky Baby to take off with astonishing ease, demonstrating that even ultralight aircraft can perform well. The plane's ingenious design, with a tubular steel fuselage and wood-and-canvas wings, helped minimize weight while ensuring a solid structure.

Flying the Sky Baby was a unique experience. Because of its tiny size, the cockpit was so narrow that the pilot had to literally squeeze into the aircraft. Despite this, the Sky Baby demonstrated impressive maneuverability during its test flights. The pilots who had the chance to fly it reported that the aircraft responded very well to controls, although it demanded great precision due to its small size and light weight. It was a real challenge to maintain stable flight, but the plane proved that even the smallest machines can be reliable in flight.

The Sky Baby was not only a technical feat, but also a statement about what was possible in light aviation. At a time when aircraft were becoming ever larger and more sophisticated, Ray Stits demonstrated that it was possible to go back to basics and build an aircraft that, despite its simplicity, could accomplish extraordinary things. This project inspired many other aircraft designers to explore the limits of lightness and miniaturization.

The Stits SA-2A Sky Baby remains a symbol of innovation and creativity in aviation. Although it was built over 70 years ago, it continues to inspire aviation enthusiasts and engineers the world over. This unique aircraft proved that lightness is not an obstacle to flight, but a quality which, when properly exploited, can achieve truly remarkable feats in the air.

# Fact 15 - First flight around the North Pole

The first flight around the North Pole was made by American explorer and aviator Richard E. Byrd, a remarkable feat that marked a milestone in the history of aerial exploration. On May 9, 1926, Byrd, accompanied by his pilot Floyd Bennett, took off from Spitsbergen, Norway, in their three-engine Fokker F.VIIa/3m aircraft named Josephine Ford. Their mission was ambitious: to reach the North Pole and back, a dangerous adventure in one of the most inhospitable regions on the planet.

The Josephine Ford aircraft was specially equipped for this expedition. Built to withstand the freezing temperatures and extreme conditions of the Far North, it also carried innovative navigation equipment for the time, including a modified sextant, used by Byrd to determine their position in flight. Navigation in the polar regions was extremely difficult due to the magnetic fields that disrupt compasses, making Byrd's precision all the more crucial to the mission's success.

The flight lasted around 15 hours, including some 13 hours in the air. Byrd and Bennett flew over the North Pole at an estimated altitude of 1,500 metres. During their flight, they had to contend with high winds, freezing temperatures and mechanical problems that tested their endurance and determination. On their return to Spitsbergen, they were greeted as heroes, and their flight was hailed as a technological achievement and a milestone in polar exploration.

However, the flight was not without controversy. Some historians and experts later questioned the accuracy of Byrd's navigation, suggesting that he might not have reached the pole precisely. Despite these debates, Byrd and Bennett's flight undeniably helped advance understanding of the challenges of flying in the polar regions, and inspired other explorers to push the boundaries of aerial exploration even further.

Today, Richard E. Byrd's feat is recognized as a pioneering milestone in the history of aviation. His flight around the North Pole demonstrated that aviation could not only overcome the most formidable geographical obstacles, but also open up new vistas for scientific exploration. The Josephine Ford, the aircraft of this incredible adventure, remains a symbol of the courage and innovation that characterized the early decades of modern aviation.

# Fact 16 - The airplane with folding wings

One of the most innovative aircraft designed for naval operations is the Grumman F6F Hellcat, a World War II shipborne fighter. What makes this aircraft particularly remarkable are its foldable wings, an essential feature for maximizing space on aircraft carriers. The F6F Hellcat was designed by Grumman Aircraft Engineering Corporation and entered service in 1943. With its foldable wings, it could be stored more efficiently on aircraft carriers, enabling more aircraft to be loaded in a limited space.

The F6F Hellcat's folding wing mechanism was both simple and ingenious. The wings folded up and down along the fuselage, significantly reducing the aircraft's wingspan. This system, operated manually by pilots and ground crew, was robust and fast, which was crucial for naval air operations where time and efficiency were of the essence. This feature not only enabled more aircraft to be carried aboard carriers, but also protected them from damage during maneuvers and combat.

The Grumman F6F Hellcat wasn't the first aircraft to feature folding wings, but it was one of the most successful and widely used. With over 12,000 built, the Hellcat played a crucial role in the Pacific theater during the Second World War. Its ability to take off quickly from a carrier, engage the enemy and return to the ship while occupying a minimum of space made it an invaluable asset to the US Navy. The folding wing system thus contributed to its operational efficiency and success in air battles.

Beyond the Second World War, folding wing technology continued to be used and perfected in naval aviation. It was adopted by many other aircraft, enabling navies around the world to maximize the use of their aircraft carriers. The F6F Hellcat, with its folding wings, set a standard that continues to this day in the design of embarked aircraft.

The impact of the Grumman F6F Hellcat and its ingenious folding wing system goes far beyond war. Not only did this aircraft make aviation history for its combat performance, it also demonstrated the importance of innovation in optimizing military operations. The Hellcat's folding wings have become a symbol of the ability to adapt aeronautical technologies to the specific needs of armed forces, while opening up new perspectives for modern naval aviation.

# Fact 17 - First airplane to land on water

The aircraft that revolutionized aviation by being the first to land on water was the Curtiss NC-4, a seaplane designed by American engineer Glenn Curtiss. In 1919, this aircraft made history by becoming the first aircraft to cross the Atlantic with stopovers, demonstrating the viability of transoceanic flights. But long before this feat, the Curtiss NC-4 had already distinguished itself by its unique ability to land and take off on water, an innovation that opened up new prospects for maritime aviation.

The Curtiss NC-4 was a hulled seaplane, a feature that set it apart from conventional aircraft of the time. Its wooden hull, specially designed to float, enabled it to land directly on the water, offering unprecedented flexibility. This type of design was ideal for reconnaissance missions, sea rescues and coastal patrols, where the presence of a traditional landing strip was often impossible. The Curtiss NC-4 was equipped with four Liberty engines, each developing 400 horsepower, enabling it to fly long distances while carrying a significant payload.

The Curtiss NC-4's most famous flight took place in May 1919, when it made the first multi-leg transatlantic crossing, linking the USA to Portugal via the Azores. On this voyage, the aircraft demonstrated its ability to land safely on the ocean for refueling, a feat that had never been accomplished before. The flight required meticulous planning, and tested and validated the aircraft's ability to operate in difficult sea conditions, proving its effectiveness as a seaplane.

The design of the Curtiss NC-4 had a lasting impact on aviation. It inspired the development of other seaplanes, which played a crucial role in exploration, communications and military operations throughout the 20th century. Seaplanes became essential for countries with vast coastlines or numerous inland water bodies, their ability to take off and land on water giving them an incomparable strategic advantage.

The Curtiss NC-4 remains a pioneer of maritime aviation, symbolizing the ingenuity and daring of the early days of aviation. Its ability to land on water opened up a new dimension in aeronautics, overcoming the limitations imposed by the need for land-based runways. This historic aircraft continues to inspire, reminding us of the daring beginnings of aviation and the importance of innovation in conquering new horizons.

# Fact 18 - A plane designed to fly through thunderstorms

One of the most fascinating and specialized aircraft ever built is the Lockheed Martin WC-130J, a plane designed for a unique and perilous mission: to fly through storms and hurricanes. Used primarily by the US Air Force's Hurricane Hunters squadron, this rugged aircraft is equipped to fly directly into the eye of the most violent storms, collecting vital data for weather forecasting.

The WC-130J is a modified version of the C-130 Hercules military transport aircraft. What sets it apart is its specialized equipment for meteorological reconnaissance missions. The aircraft is equipped with probes, Doppler radars and various instruments that measure atmospheric pressure, temperature, wind speed and humidity inside storms. These data are crucial to understanding the structure and intensity of hurricanes, enabling us to predict their trajectory and take measures to protect populations.

Flying into a hurricane is one of the riskiest missions in aviation. The WC-130J's pilots have to cope with extreme turbulence, winds sometimes exceeding 200 km/h, and virtually zero visibility. Yet, thanks to the aircraft's robustness and the expertise of its crew, these missions are carried out successfully, providing information that satellites and other surveillance tools cannot obtain with the same precision.

The WC-130J is designed to withstand the harshest conditions. It is built to withstand intense aerodynamic forces, and its communication systems are reinforced to remain operational even in the heart of storms. The cockpit is also equipped with multiple screens and display systems that enable pilots to navigate with precision in these extreme conditions, using real-time data provided by the on-board instruments.

The Lockheed Martin WC-130J is a true unsung aviation hero. Each flight through a hurricane brings valuable information that saves lives and helps to better understand these devastating natural phenomena. This unique aircraft is the fruit of years of research and development, combining cutting-edge engineering and human courage to face nature's most formidable forces.

# Fact 19 - First computer-controlled airplane

The advent of computer-controlled aircraft revolutionized modern aviation, and the first plane to achieve this feat was the Boeing 720, modified to become the Crested Butte, an unmanned aircraft controlled entirely by computer. This daring project, carried out by NASA and the Federal Aviation Administration (FAA) in the 1980s, was designed to test safety technologies, particularly for simulated crashes, in order to improve the safety of commercial flights.

The Crested Butte, a modified Boeing 720 airliner, was equipped with cutting-edge technology for its time. Traditional flight controls were replaced by a computer system capable of piloting the aircraft without direct human intervention. This system used sensors, advanced software and a radio link to receive instructions and execute them with a precision never seen before. The flight, entirely computer-controlled, was completed on December 1, 1984, marking a milestone in the development of automated aviation systems.

The flight of the Crested Butte was particularly spectacular because it was a full-scale safety test. The aim was to simulate a crash to gather valuable data on how an aircraft behaves during a controlled impact. The plane was flown to a desert test site in California, where it was intentionally crashed to test the effectiveness of new safety features. This test, dubbed the Controlled Impact Demonstration, yielded crucial information that has contributed to the improvement of construction materials and evacuation procedures in modern aircraft.

This project marked a turning point in aviation by proving that aircraft could be controlled autonomously by computers, paving the way for today's drone and automated flight system technologies. The idea that aircraft could fly without a human pilot on board was revolutionary at the time, and led to significant advances in automated navigation systems, used today not only in military but also in civil aviation.

The Boeing 720 Crested Butte is therefore not only a symbol of technological innovation, but also a precursor of the automated flight systems found in aviation today. This first computer-controlled flight demonstrated the infinite possibilities offered by the technologies of the time, laying the foundations for the automated flight control systems that are now essential to ensuring the safety and efficiency of modern flight operations.

# Fact 20 - The fastest unmanned aircraft

The fastest unmanned aircraft ever built is the North American X-43A, an experimental hypersonic craft developed by NASA. This unmanned aircraft, also known as Hyper-X, made aviation history by reaching a record speed of Mach 9.6, or around 11,265 km/h, during its flight on November 16, 2004. The X-43A thus demonstrated the potential of scramjet propulsion, a revolutionary technology enabling flight at speeds few other aircraft have achieved.

The X-43A was powered by a scramjet (Supersonic Combustion Ramjet) engine, a technology that uses oxygen from the atmosphere for combustion, eliminating the need to carry liquid oxygen like traditional rocket engines. This unique propulsion works only at supersonic speeds, and the X-43A was dropped from a carrier aircraft, a B-52, before igniting its engine to reach hypersonic speeds. The flight lasted around 10 seconds at maximum speed, but proved that scramjet aircraft could one day revolutionize air and space travel.

The X-43A's design was particularly innovative, with an elongated, tapering shape designed to minimize aerodynamic drag at extremely high speeds. The aircraft measured around 3.7 meters in length, a modest size for a machine capable of such performance. Its structure was mainly made of composite materials, capable of withstanding the extremely high temperatures generated by air friction at these speeds. Each flight of the X-43A contributed to a better understanding of the challenges of hypersonic flight.

NASA's Hyper-X program, of which the X-43A was a part, aimed to explore the technologies required for hypersonic flight in the Earth's atmosphere. Data collected during X-43A flights provided valuable information on fluid dynamics, high-speed combustion and high-temperature materials. This information is essential for the future development of civil and military aircraft capable of flying at hypersonic speeds, potentially paving the way for transcontinental flights in under an hour.

The North American X-43A remains an icon of experimental aviation, pushing back the boundaries of what is possible in the realm of air speed. This unmanned speed record remains unsurpassed to this day, making the X-43A a spectacular example of technological innovation and mankind's relentless quest to explore the frontiers of the possible in the skies and beyond.

# Fact 21 - The first successful night flight

The first successful night flight is a milestone in aviation history, and was achieved by American aviator Calbraith Perry Rodgers on November 11, 1910. Rodgers, who had already made history by making the first crossing of the United States in an airplane, set himself an even bolder challenge: to fly at night. This flight, aboard his Wright Model B, showed that it was possible to navigate in the dark, a significant advance for aviation.

Flying at night in those days represented a major technical and human challenge. Navigation instruments were rudimentary, and there were no modern navigational aids such as airfield lights or radio navigation systems. Rodgers had to rely on his flying skills, experience and meticulous preparation. The flight took place in Chicago, under clear but dark skies, and lasted around 25 minutes, a short time but enough to demonstrate the feasibility of night flying.

This night flight was accomplished in conditions very different from those we know today. The Wright Model B was an open biplane, with no closed cockpit to protect the pilot from the wind or cold of the night. The plane was powered by a 35-horsepower propeller engine, a modest output that limited speed and altitude, but sufficient to maintain stable flight. Navigation was mainly by sight, following the lights of the city below, a risky but effective method.

Rodgers' successful flight paved the way for the exploration of night flying in commercial and military aviation. He demonstrated that, despite the darkness, it was possible to fly an aircraft safely, a skill that would soon be essential for mail transport missions, and later for passenger flights. The first scheduled night flights soon followed, making possible continuous air transport, day and night, across the country and, later, around the world.

Calbraith Perry Rodgers didn't just achieve a technical feat; he inspired other pilots to push back the boundaries of what was considered possible in aviation. His successful night flight became a cornerstone of aviation, showing that even in the dark, with the right equipment and the right spirit, the sky could be conquered. Today, night flying is routine, but it has its roots in the courageous early attempts of pioneers like Rodgers.

# Fact 22 - The plane that can land vertically

One of the most revolutionary aircraft in aviation history is the Harrier Jump Jet, known for its unique ability to take off and land vertically. Developed in the early 1960s by the British company Hawker Siddeley, the Harrier introduced a technology that transformed air operations, particularly for the armed forces, by enabling take-offs and landings in very restricted areas, without the need for a traditional runway.

The secret of this feat lies in the Pegasus engine, a turbofan with steerable ejection nozzles. These nozzles can be rotated downwards to direct vertical thrust, enabling the aircraft to take off and land like a helicopter. Once airborne, the nozzles rotate backwards to allow the Harrier to fly horizontally like a conventional aircraft. This unique combination of vertical and horizontal flight makes the Harrier an extremely versatile aircraft, capable of operating from small platforms such as aircraft carriers or improvised combat zones.

The Harrier was first used in combat during the Falklands War in 1982, where its ability to take off from and land on British aircraft carriers was crucial. Harrier aircraft were able to intervene quickly and effectively in aerial combat, demonstrating their strategic value. Their ability to land vertically also enabled pilots to land safely even on moving ships or rough terrain, where a conventional aircraft would have been unable to land.

This unique Harrier capability has also influenced the design of other military and civil aircraft, including future vertical take-off and landing (VTOL) fighters. The Harrier's legacy can be seen in aircraft such as the F-35B Lightning II, which uses advanced propulsion technology to deliver similar capabilities. The Harrier remains a pioneer in this field, however, and its bold design continues to be celebrated for pushing the boundaries of what aircraft can achieve.

The Harrier Jump Jet is not only a technical feat, but also a symbol of human ingenuity, capable of reinventing the way aircraft interact with the environment. By enabling air operations in previously inaccessible areas, it has opened up new possibilities for both military and civilian missions, proving that innovation can literally redefine the rules of the game in aviation.

# Fact 23 - First flight with a giant propeller

The first flight using a giant propeller was achieved by the Caproni Ca.60 Transaereo, an experimental aircraft designed by Italian engineer Giovanni Battista Caproni in 1921. This ambitious project, nicknamed the "Noviplano", was designed to carry up to 100 passengers over long transatlantic distances, a bold vision for its time. The airplane, a veritable giant of the air, was equipped with eight engines and three sets of triplane wings, each with large propellers to provide the thrust required for this enormous aircraft.

The Caproni Ca.60's giant propeller, measuring over 4 meters in diameter, was an essential component in generating enough force to lift this 30-ton aircraft into the air. Each propeller was coupled to a Liberty L-12, a 400 hp V12 engine, making it one of the most powerful aircraft of its time. These propellers, placed in front of the engines, were designed to maximize traction and provide the necessary lift for this colossal aircraft.

The first and only flight of the Caproni Ca.60 took place on March 4, 1921, over Lake Maggiore in Italy. Unfortunately, the flight was short-lived. After a successful takeoff, the aircraft was unable to stabilize its flight and crashed into the lake shortly after leaving the water. Although there were no casualties, the accident marked the end of the project. The giant propeller and the whole concept were too far ahead of their time, and the technical challenges of building such a large aircraft were still insurmountable at the time.

Despite this failure, the Caproni Ca.60 remains a fascinating milestone in aviation history. It demonstrated the limits and possibilities of large-scale aviation, inspiring even bigger and more ambitious aircraft projects decades later. The use of giant propellers to generate powerful lift was a concept explored by many engineers in the quest for aircraft capable of carrying large loads over long distances.

The Caproni Ca.60 Transaereo is often evoked as a symbol of the daring and innovation of aviation pioneers. Although its flight was brief, it paved the way for new ideas about what commercial aviation could one day achieve. The giant propeller that was to carry this aircraft over the oceans remains a testament to the human ingenuity and grandiose dreams that shaped aviation history.

# Fact 24 - The silent plane to spy on the enemy

One of the most mysterious and innovative aircraft in history is the Lockheed U-2, a reconnaissance plane designed to spy on the enemy without being detected. Developed in great secrecy by Lockheed's famous Skunk Works division, under the direction of Clarence "Kelly" Johnson, the U-2 entered service in the 1950s. Its main mission: to fly at high altitude over enemy territory, in particular the Soviet Union, and gather strategic intelligence, while evading radar and air defenses.

The U-2 was designed to fly at an incredible altitude of over 21,000 meters, well beyond the range of surface-to-air missiles and interceptors of the time. To accomplish this, it not only had to be extremely light and aerodynamic, but also incredibly quiet to reduce the risk of acoustic detection. Aircraft noise was minimized thanks to a low-noise engine, a long, slim fuselage and particularly long, narrow wings, which enabled stable flight at high altitudes with minimal drag.

The aircraft was equipped with state-of-the-art cameras and sensors, capable of capturing detailed images and collecting electronic data on ongoing military activities. The U-2's first operational flight took place in 1956, and its missions over the Soviet Union soon provided crucial information on the country's military installations and nuclear capabilities. These flights, though risky, were essential for the United States during the Cold War, providing valuable insight into enemy activities without triggering direct confrontation.

One of the most impressive aspects of the U-2 was its ability to remain undetected. Flying at an altitude where no other aircraft could operate, the U-2 was able to carry out reconnaissance missions for several years without being intercepted. However, in 1960, a U-2 piloted by Francis Gary Powers was shot down by a Soviet missile during a mission over the Soviet Union, revealing to the world the existence of this ultra-secret reconnaissance program.

The Lockheed U-2 marked a turning point in military aviation and intelligence gathering. It proved that stealth and high altitude could be decisive assets in information warfare. Although other more advanced reconnaissance aircraft followed, the U-2 remains an icon of the Cold War era, symbolizing aviation's ability to play a decisive role in conflicts without ever firing a shot.

# Fact 25 - First flight with a single engine

The first successful single-engine flight dates back to December 17, 1903, when the Wright brothers took off their airplane, the Wright Flyer, in Kitty Hawk, North Carolina. This historic flight, which marked the beginning of modern aviation, was powered by a 12-horsepower gasoline engine, specially designed by the Wright brothers to power their plane. The Wright Flyer was a lightweight biplane, made mainly of wood and canvas, with a wingspan of 12.3 meters. This single, light and simple engine was sufficient to provide the power needed to keep the plane in the air.

The Wright Flyer engine was an innovation in itself. At a time when engine technology was still in its infancy, the Wright brothers had to design and build an engine themselves to meet the demands of their aviation project. They collaborated with their mechanic, Charlie Taylor, to create this four-cylinder, water-cooled engine, which weighed around 77 kilograms. The engine, mounted to the right of the pilot, was linked to two propellers by a chain, an arrangement that ensured balanced power distribution for flight.

The Wright Flyer's flight lasted just 12 seconds and covered a distance of 37 meters, but it was a resounding demonstration that powered flight was possible. The fact that this flight was accomplished with a single engine was a technical feat, given the challenges of the time. The Wright brothers not only succeeded in getting their plane airborne, they also managed to control it in flight, thanks to their ingenious three-axis control system, another innovation that was to become a standard in aviation.

The use of a single engine for this first flight laid the foundations for the development of many other single-engine aircraft, which would dominate light aviation for decades to come. This mechanical simplicity made these aircraft more accessible and easier to maintain, helping to popularize aviation among hobbyists and professional pilots alike. The concept of the single-engine aircraft proved that it was possible to fly safely and efficiently with a minimum of mechanical complexity.

The flight of the Wright Flyer remains an emblematic moment in aviation history. This first powered flight, accomplished with a single engine, paved the way for all the aeronautical advances that followed. It is a reminder that even with modest means and limited resources, innovation and perseverance can lead to extraordinary achievements, laying the foundations for all that aviation has subsequently become.

# Fact 26 - The plane that flew over Everest

In 1933, a historic aeronautical feat was accomplished when two British pilots, the Marquis of Clydesdale (Douglas Douglas-Hamilton) and David McIntyre, successfully flew over Mount Everest, the world's highest mountain, in two Westland PV-3 aircraft. This daring mission, organized by the Royal Geographical Society and financed by the commander and adventurer Sir Philip Sassoon, marked the first time that aircraft had flown over the snow-covered peaks of the Himalayas, opening up new perspectives for high-altitude aviation.

The Westland PV-3s were specially modified for this unique flight. These single-engine, open-cockpit aircraft, powered by Bristol Pegasus engines, were fitted with supplementary oxygen and heaters to enable pilots to survive the extreme conditions encountered at altitudes above 10,000 meters. The engines have also been adapted to operate more efficiently in rarefied air, where atmospheric density is much lower than near sea level, making lift and thrust more difficult to achieve.

On April 3, 1933, the two pilots took off from Purnea, India, and headed for Mount Everest. After a difficult flight through high winds and freezing temperatures, they reached the summit of Mount Everest, flying some 300 meters above the snow-capped peak. This historic flight captured the world's first aerial images of the summit, revealing spectacular and previously unknown views of the Himalayas, and provided invaluable data for mapping and geographical understanding of the region.

This flight was not only a technical feat, but also a human adventure. The pilots had to cope with extremely difficult flying conditions, with temperatures dropping well below zero, a lack of oxygen, and the need to maneuver through unpredictable updrafts. Their success not only proved that high-altitude flight was possible, but also inspired new aerial explorations in extreme environments.

The flight over Everest in 1933 paved the way for even more ambitious aerial exploration missions, demonstrating that aviation could conquer even the planet's most hostile environments. Today, this flight is celebrated as one of the greatest aviation feats of its time, a reminder of the ingenuity and courage of the pioneers who pushed back the boundaries of what was possible to explore the world from the air.

# Fact 27 - First high-altitude reconnaissance aircraft

The first aircraft designed specifically for high-altitude reconnaissance was the Lockheed U-2, a legendary aircraft developed in the 1950s to meet U.S. intelligence needs during the Cold War. Known by its code name "Dragon Lady," the U-2 was designed to fly at extreme altitudes, up to 21,000 meters, well beyond the range of air defenses at the time. This unique capability enabled the USA to gather vital information on the Soviet Union and other inaccessible regions, flying at altitudes where it was almost invisible and invulnerable to attack.

The U-2 was designed by Lockheed's Skunk Works division, under the direction of engineer Clarence "Kelly" Johnson. Its lightweight design, with a predominantly aluminum structure and long, slender wings, enabled it to stay aloft for long periods with low fuel consumption. The Pratt & Whitney J57 engine, modified for this type of flight, provided the power needed to reach high altitudes while maintaining a low heat signature, thus reducing the probability of detection by enemy radars.

The U-2 made its first operational flight in 1956. It immediately proved its worth by collecting high-quality images and other essential information on Soviet military installations. This information was crucial in assessing the USSR's nuclear capabilities, and enabled strategic decisions to be made during the Cold War. The U-2 also flew over other sensitive regions, such as Cuba during the 1962 missile crisis, providing essential photographic evidence for political decision-makers.

Despite its successes, the U-2 was not without risks. In 1960, a U-2 piloted by Francis Gary Powers was shot down over the Soviet Union, leading to a major diplomatic crisis between the USA and the USSR. This incident revealed the existence of this ultra-secret reconnaissance program and highlighted the dangers faced by reconnaissance pilots. Nevertheless, the U-2 continued to be used for critical missions for decades, thanks to its unrivalled high-altitude surveillance capabilities.

The Lockheed U-2 remains one of the most iconic reconnaissance aircraft in aviation history. Its ingenious design and extraordinary performance not only changed the course of the Cold War, but also laid the foundations for modern reconnaissance aviation.

# Fact 28 - The commercial aircraft that flies the farthest

The commercial aircraft capable of flying the farthest is the Boeing 777-200LR, designed for ultra-long-haul routes. The "LR" in its designation stands for "Longer Range," underlining its exceptional ability to cover impressive distances non-stop. This model, introduced in 2006, holds the world record for the longest commercial flight, with a maximum range of 15,843 kilometers, making it possible to connect virtually any major city in the world without the need for refueling.

The Boeing 777-200LR has been designed to meet the growing demand from airlines for direct flights between distant destinations. Thanks to additional fuel tanks, more powerful engines and optimized aerodynamics, this aircraft is capable of flying for more than 18 hours at a time. In 2005, before entering commercial service, the 777-200LR set a record by flying non-stop from Hong Kong to London in an easterly direction, covering a distance of 21,601 kilometers in 22 hours and 42 minutes, well beyond its normal range, on a round-the-world route.

The architecture of the 777-200LR is specially adapted for long-haul flights. It is powered by two GE90-115B engines, the world's most powerful commercial jet engines, each capable of generating up to 115,300 pounds of thrust. This power, combined with increased fuel capacity and a lightweight composite structure, enables the 777-200LR to carry a maximum load while maintaining extended range, even in adverse weather conditions or on routes optimized for fuel efficiency.

Airlines are using the 777-200LR to connect cities such as New York and Singapore, Sydney and Dallas, or Doha and Los Angeles, routes that previously required a stopover. For passengers, this means less time spent in transit and more direct travel. The aircraft's interior is also designed to maximize comfort on these very long flights, with advanced pressurization systems, controlled humidity and seats designed for rest.

The Boeing 777-200LR symbolizes the pinnacle of aeronautical engineering when it comes to long-haul flights. Not only has it pushed back the limits of how far a commercial aircraft can fly non-stop, it has also redefined what it means to travel to the other side of the world. Thanks to this aircraft, journeys that once seemed inconceivable have become routine, changing the way the world is connected by air.

# Fact 29 - The longest flight of a glider

The longest flight ever made by a glider was accomplished on December 2, 2018 by pilots Jim Payne and Tim Gardner aboard the Perlan 2, an experimental glider designed to explore the limits of the Earth's atmosphere. On this historic flight, the Perlan 2 covered a distance of 3,008 kilometers in a straight line across the skies of Argentina, setting a world record for the longest distance ever covered by an unpowered glider.

The Perlan 2 is a unique glider, specially designed for high-altitude flying. Its lightweight yet robust structure enables it to soar in updrafts known as mountain waves, which form when the wind blows over mountain ranges such as the Andes. By exploiting these waves, the Perlan 2 can reach altitudes where air is extremely scarce, and where powered aircraft have difficulty flying. This record-breaking flight demonstrated not only the efficiency of the Perlan 2's design, but also the pilots' skills in exploiting natural phenomena to extend their flight.

The Perlan 2 aircraft, which was built for scientific research into extreme flight conditions, is engineless, making this feat all the more impressive. During this record-breaking flight, the pilots had to constantly adjust their trajectory to stay in the updrafts while navigating through areas of intense turbulence. The physical and mental endurance required to pilot a glider for hours on end, without any motorized assistance, underlines the difficulty of this feat.

The flight also collected valuable scientific data on the atmosphere, particularly on the upper layers of the stratosphere, where conditions are similar to those found on Mars. The information gathered during this flight is helping to better understand weather and climate phenomena, and could one day contribute to the design of aerial vehicles for space exploration.

The Perlan 2, with its flight of 3,008 kilometers, not only broke a record, but also pushed back the limits of what was thought possible for a glider. This feat represents a perfect fusion of cutting-edge technology and the skilful use of natural forces, demonstrating that, even without a motor, man can explore inaccessible regions of the sky. This flight will go down in the annals of aviation as a testament to the incredible potential of motorless flight.

# Fact 30 - The open cockpit aircraft

One of the most emblematic aircraft from the pioneering days of aviation is the Sopwith Camel, a British biplane fighter from the First World War. This type of aircraft was equipped with an open cockpit, a feature common to many aircraft of the period. The Sopwith Camel was introduced in 1917 and became one of the most feared aircraft of the conflict, thanks to its exceptional maneuverability and firepower, but it offered little comfort or protection for its pilot, who was exposed to the elements on every mission.

The open cockpit of the Sopwith Camel meant that the pilot was directly exposed to the wind, rain and intense cold at high altitude. Pilots had to wear heavy clothing, goggles and helmets to protect themselves from the harsh conditions. The lack of weather protection made flying even more perilous, especially in winter or on high-altitude flights where temperatures dropped well below freezing. Despite this, pilots of the time often saw the open cockpit as an advantage, offering better visibility in aerial combat.

The Sopwith Camel was equipped with two synchronized machine guns, firing through the propeller, making it a formidable aircraft in aerial duels. However, its design made piloting particularly tricky. With a powerful rotary engine and an offset center of gravity, the Camel had a tendency to pull violently to the left, requiring constant attention from the pilot. This characteristic, combined with the open cockpit, meant that flying the Sopwith Camel demanded not only technical skill, but also great physical endurance.

Despite these challenges, the Sopwith Camel made aviation history with an impressive record of aerial victories. It is credited with shooting down over 1,200 enemy aircraft during the war, making it one of the most effective fighters of its day. Its open cockpit, while primitive by modern standards, was an integral part of the flying experience of the time and helped forge the romantic image of early fighter pilots, often referred to as the "knights of the sky."

Today, the Sopwith Camel is regarded as a symbol of the heroic beginnings of military aviation. Its open cockpit represents a time when flying was still a perilous novelty, when every mission was a challenge against the elements as much as against the enemy. This type of aircraft is a reminder that aviation, in its early days, demanded extraordinary courage and resilience from those who dared to venture into the air.

# Fact 31 - The plane that crossed the Pacific Ocean

One of aviation's most daring feats was achieved by Charles Kingsford Smith and his crew in 1928, when they crossed the Pacific Ocean aboard the Southern Cross. This aircraft, a three-engine Fokker F.VII/3m, became the first to make a non-stop flight over the Pacific, linking Oakland, California, to Brisbane, Australia. This historic flight took more than 83 hours, spread over three legs, marking a significant advance in air connectivity between continents.

The Southern Cross was a robust aircraft, originally designed to carry passengers and freight. For this transpacific mission, it was modified to carry more fuel, at the expense of payload, to allow sufficient range to cross vast stretches of ocean without refueling. The plane's three Wright Whirlwind engines were renowned for their reliability, a crucial factor for such a perilous flight where any mechanical problem could have been fatal.

The flight began on May 31, 1928, when Kingsford Smith, accompanied by co-pilot Charles Ulm, navigator Harry Lyon and wireless operator James Warner, took off from Oakland. The first leg took them to Honolulu, through often overcast skies and over an endless ocean. After a short break in Hawaii to rest and refuel, the crew resumed their flight to Suva, Fiji, before finally landing in Brisbane on June 9. This flight of over 11,000 kilometers captivated the whole world, demonstrating for the first time that the Pacific could be crossed by air.

The crossing of the Pacific Ocean by the Southern Cross was not only a technical feat, but also a feat of navigation and courage. At a time when navigation instruments were rudimentary and radio was still a developing technology, the crew had to rely on their skill, determination and composure to succeed. The flight was punctuated by moments of uncertainty, including long periods without radio contact and unexpected tropical storm crossings.

The success of the Southern Cross opened up new horizons for commercial aviation and communication between continents. Kingsford Smith became an international hero, and his historic flight demonstrated that aviation could connect even the most remote corners of the globe. This flight marked the beginning of a new era in aviation, proving that oceans, once considered impassable barriers, could now be successfully flown over, forever changing the way people travel and connect across the globe.

# Fact 32 - First non-stop round-the-world flight

The first non-stop round-the-world flight was made in 1986 by American pilots Dick Rutan and Jeana Yeager aboard Voyager, a revolutionary aircraft specially designed for this daring mission. On December 14, 1986, Voyager took off from Edwards Air Force Base in California, marking the beginning of an unprecedented aeronautical adventure. After nine days, three minutes and forty-four seconds of uninterrupted flight, the aircraft completed its circumnavigation of the globe on December 23, having covered more than 42,000 kilometers without ever landing or refueling.

The Voyager was designed by Burt Rutan, a renowned aeronautical engineer, to maximize flight autonomy while minimizing fuel consumption. The aircraft, made mainly of lightweight composite materials, had an impressive wingspan of 33.8 meters, but weighed just 1,020 kilograms empty. It carried 3,180 liters of fuel, or 72% of its total take-off weight. The aircraft's unique configuration, with two slim fuselages and a long central wing, was optimized to fly at low fuel consumption while carrying a large amount of fuel.

During their flight, Fact and Yeager faced many challenges, including severe turbulence, unpredictable weather conditions and fatigue due to the long duration of the flight. The two pilots took it in turns to keep the plane aloft in a cramped cockpit, with no real chance to rest. Voyager had no heating or pressurization system, which made the flight even more demanding, especially during high-altitude passages where temperatures were freezing.

Despite these difficulties, the Voyager flight was a resounding success and a milestone in aviation history. The aircraft landed at Edwards Air Force Base with only a few liters of fuel remaining, proving the precision of planning and the reliability of the aircraft's design. This feat attracted worldwide attention and was hailed as an extraordinary demonstration of human ingenuity and pilot determination.

Today, Voyager is on display at the National Air and Space Museum in Washington, D.C., where it is honored as one of the greatest feats of modern aviation. Rutan and Yeager's non-stop flight around the world remains a source of inspiration, illustrating the limits that man can push back with technology, endurance and vision. This daring flight paved the way for new innovations in aviation, showing that even the most extreme challenges can be overcome.

# Fact 33 - The plane that can take off without a runway

One of the most innovative aircraft in aviation history is the Hawker Harrier, an aircraft designed to take off vertically, eliminating the need for a conventional runway. Developed in the early 1960s by Hawker Siddeley in the UK, the Harrier became the first operational vertical take-off and landing (VTOL) jet aircraft. This unique capability revolutionized air operations, particularly for military forces, enabling aircraft to take off from unprepared terrain, close combat zones and warships.

The Harrier uses a Rolls-Royce Pegasus jet engine, specially designed for this task. This engine is equipped with four steerable nozzles that direct thrust downwards for vertical take-off. Once airborne, the nozzles can be progressively rotated backwards to enable the Harrier to fly horizontally like a conventional aircraft. This innovative system enables the Harrier to take off and land in confined spaces where no other jet could operate.

The Harrier was first used in combat during the Falklands War in 1982, where its ability to take off from the decks of British aircraft carriers, which were too small for traditional aircraft, played a crucial role. Harriers were able to intervene rapidly in support of ground troops, demonstrating the strategic advantage of their VTOL capability. Their operational flexibility enabled them to carry out both offensive and defensive missions, even in difficult logistical conditions.

In addition to its military capabilities, the Harrier also made its mark for its role in technological development. The VTOL concept inspired a great deal of aviation research and innovation, leading to the development of other aircraft capable of taking off and landing without runways. The Harrier proved that aviation was not limited to airports and long runways, but could adapt to the most varied and demanding environments.

Today, the Harrier is recognized as a pioneer of VTOL aviation, and although more modern aircraft have since taken its place, it remains a symbol of innovation and flexibility in aviation. Its ability to take off without a runway not only changed the way aircraft are used in combat, but also opened up new possibilities for aviation in both civilian and military contexts.

# Fact 34 - First plane with electric motor

The first electrically-powered aircraft to make a successful flight was the MB-E1, designed by German engineer Fred Militky and aviator Heino Brditschka in 1973. This light aircraft, derived from the HB-3 powered glider, made aviation history with a flight powered entirely by an electric motor, marking a significant step forward in the search for alternative, environmentally-friendly propulsion solutions.

The MB-E1 was equipped with a Bosch 10 kW electric motor, powered by a nickel-cadmium battery. This motor, relatively modest by combustion aircraft standards, enabled the aircraft to take off, fly and land autonomously over a distance of 7 minutes. Although the flight was short, it demonstrated the feasibility of using electric power for aerial propulsion, paving the way for future innovations in green aviation.

The historic flight of the MB-E1 took place on October 21, 1973, on a small airfield near Vienna, Austria. Although the aircraft's performance was limited by the capacity of the batteries available at the time, this first flight showed that it was possible to design aircraft capable of flying without direct $CO_2$ emissions. This success encouraged other researchers and engineers to pursue the development of electric propulsion technologies, gradually overcoming the challenges of battery energy density.

The innovation of the MB-E1 lay in its simplicity and efficiency. The lightweight, reliable electric motor produced less vibration and noise than traditional combustion engines, offering a quieter, smoother flying experience. What's more, the absence of liquid fuel made the aircraft safer in the event of an accident, a significant advantage for the first tests of this new technology. The MB-E1 flight proved that electric motors could be a viable alternative for light aircraft, particularly for short flights and training aircraft.

The MB-E1 was a pioneer in the field of electric aircraft, inspiring decades of research and development aimed at making aviation more sustainable. Today, as environmental concerns become ever more pressing, the MB-E1's legacy is more relevant than ever. It symbolizes the beginnings of a quiet revolution in aviation, where electric power could one day supplant fossil fuels as the main source of aircraft propulsion.

# Fact 35 - The widest airplane ever built

The widest aircraft ever built is the Stratolaunch, designed as a launch platform for rockets carrying satellites into orbit. With a wingspan of 117 meters, it far exceeds that of any other aircraft, including the legendary Hughes H-4 Hercules (better known as the "Spruce Goose"). Built by Stratolaunch Systems, a company founded by Microsoft co-creator Paul Allen, this colossal aircraft made its maiden flight on April 13, 2019, marking an impressive milestone in aviation history.

The Stratolaunch is powered by six Pratt & Whitney PW4056 engines, the same as those used on the Boeing 747, and has two parallel fuselages connected by a massive central wing. This unusual design allows large payloads to be carried under the center wing, between the two fuselages. The aircraft is capable of carrying rockets to high altitudes, where they can be launched to minimize fuel consumption and the cost of launching from the ground.

The idea behind Stratolaunch is to make satellite launches more flexible and less costly. By using an aircraft to carry rockets to an altitude of around 10,000 meters, launches can be carried out from virtually anywhere, avoiding the geographical and meteorological constraints that affect ground launch sites. This also reduces launch risks, as the aircraft can return to base in the event of a problem before the rocket is released.

The development of the Stratolaunch represented an immense technical challenge. With a wingspan almost as long as a soccer field, this aircraft weighs around 226 tonnes empty, and can reach a maximum take-off weight of 590 tonnes with its payload. Its massive size requires specific infrastructures for storage and maintenance, and it took several years of design and testing before the plane could finally fly.

The Stratolaunch embodies large-scale innovation in modern aviation. Although designed primarily for space missions, it demonstrates how aircraft design can push the boundaries of what is possible, both in terms of size and functionality. This giant aircraft, with its imposing silhouette and record wingspan, symbolizes the relentless pursuit of exploration and technological innovation, opening up new perspectives for the future of aviation and space exploration.

# Fact 36 - First composite aircraft

The first aircraft built primarily from composite materials was the Rutan VariEze, an innovative lightweight aircraft designed by Burt Rutan in the 1970s. The VariEze marked a turning point in aviation by using composite materials such as fiberglass and epoxy, which offered a higher strength-to-weight ratio than traditional materials such as aluminum. This design choice resulted in a lighter, more aerodynamic and more efficient aircraft, laying the foundations for many future innovations in the aviation industry.

The Rutan VariEze was first introduced in 1975 at the Oshkosh Air Show, where it immediately attracted attention for its unique appearance and exceptional flying characteristics. The use of composite materials enabled us to design an aircraft with a "duck" structure, where the small front wings (fins) and inverted tail (rather than the main wing) play a crucial role in the aircraft's stability and control. This configuration, combined with lightweight construction, enabled the VariEze to achieve impressive performance with a small engine.

The VariEze was not only revolutionary in terms of materials, but also in terms of construction. Composites allowed greater freedom in the design of aerodynamic shapes, making it possible to create a smoother, more efficient structure. Owners could buy the VariEze in kit form and build it themselves, democratizing access to personal aviation. Many aviation enthusiasts were thus able to experiment with the construction of an aircraft in composite materials, a concept previously reserved for large aeronautical companies.

The use of composite materials in the VariEze has demonstrated that these materials can not only rival traditional metals, but even surpass them in certain aspects. Composites offer improved corrosion resistance, design flexibility and reduced weight, while maintaining high strength. These advantages were quickly recognized by the industry, and today composite materials are commonly used in the construction of modern aircraft, including airliners such as the Boeing 787 Dreamliner and Airbus A350.

The Rutan VariEze remains a symbol of innovation and change in the aviation industry. It has proved that composite materials can play a major role in aircraft design, leading to higher-performance, more fuel-efficient aircraft.

# Fact 37 - The plane with the longest wings

The aircraft with the longest wings ever built is the Stratolaunch, designed as a launch platform for rockets. With an incredible wingspan of 117 meters, this aircraft holds the world record for the longest wing, surpassing that of any other aircraft, including giants like the Airbus A380 or the Boeing 747. The Stratolaunch was designed by Stratolaunch Systems, a company founded by Microsoft co-founder Paul Allen, and made its maiden flight on April 13, 2019.

The Stratolaunch's huge wingspan is crucial to its main mission: to carry heavy payloads, such as rockets, to high altitude before launching them into orbit. The long wings enable the aircraft to generate sufficient lift to lift its 226 tonnes empty, while supporting a payload of up to 250 tonnes. This design optimizes low-altitude flight efficiency and reduces fuel consumption, an essential factor for long, complex missions.

The Stratolaunch is powered by six Pratt & Whitney PW4056 engines, usually used on Boeing 747s, and features two parallel fuselages connected by a central wing. This particular structure ensures high stability in flight, despite the colossal dimensions of the wing. What's more, the enormous wingspan provides sufficient surface area to attach several rockets or satellites, making the Stratolaunch a flexible and innovative air-launch platform.

The development of the Stratolaunch represented a considerable technical challenge, not only because of the size of the wing, but also because of the material and structural strength requirements. Engineers had to use advanced composite materials to ensure that the wing would be both lightweight and robust, capable of withstanding the forces exerted during flight and payload launch. This engineering feat reflects modern aviation's advanced technologies and commitment to pushing back the boundaries of the possible.

Today, the Stratolaunch remains a symbol of innovation in aeronautics. With its record wingspan, this aircraft redefined what was thought possible in aerial design. It represents not only a technological breakthrough, but also a new way of thinking about space exploration, where the use of aviation for orbital launches could make access to space more efficient and less costly.

# Fact 38 - First unmanned high-altitude flight

The first high-altitude unmanned flight was accomplished in 1964 by the Lockheed D-21, a reconnaissance drone designed to fly at extreme altitudes and supersonic speeds. This drone, developed during the Cold War by Lockheed's Skunk Works division, was intended for reconnaissance missions over enemy territory, notably the Soviet Union, where it could capture high-quality images without risking the pilots' lives.

The D-21 was launched from the back of a carrier aircraft, initially a modified Lockheed A-12, known as the M-21. Once airborne, the drone soared to an altitude of 27,000 meters, reaching a speed of Mach 3.3, making it virtually invulnerable to the interceptors and air defense systems of the day. Its ability to fly at such altitudes and speeds without a human pilot on board represented a major technological advance, paving the way for a new era of aerial reconnaissance.

The D-21 was equipped with sophisticated cameras to photograph strategic installations, and once its mission was accomplished, it dropped its payload into a capsule that was recovered in flight by a recovery aircraft or dropped at sea to be picked up by a ship. The drone itself was programmed to self-destruct after the mission, so as not to fall into enemy hands. This innovative approach minimized the risks to covert intelligence-gathering operations.

Although the D-21 had enormous potential, its program encountered several difficulties. The first test flight in 1966 was marked by a tragic accident when the drone collided with the carrier aircraft during launch, resulting in the loss of the M-21 and the death of a crew member. Despite these challenges, the D-21 carried out several reconnaissance missions over China, although the results were mixed due to technical problems and mission complexity.

The Lockheed D-21 remains a milestone in aviation history, marking the transition to the use of drones for high-altitude reconnaissance missions. Its development influenced the design of modern UAVs, which are now widely used in military and civilian operations. The D-21 symbolizes a milestone in the evolution of unmanned aircraft, demonstrating that it is possible to carry out crucial missions with minimal human risk.

# Fact 39 - The aircraft designed for short landings

One of the aircraft most noted for its short-landing capabilities is the de Havilland Canada DHC-6 Twin Otter, a versatile aircraft designed specifically to operate on short, unprepared runways. Introduced in 1965, this twin-engine propeller-driven aircraft was designed to meet the needs of remote regions with limited airport infrastructure. The Twin Otter quickly established itself as the aircraft of choice for operations in difficult environments, from the tropics to the poles.

The DHC-6 Twin Otter is powered by Pratt & Whitney PT6A engines, giving it sufficient power to take off and land over very short distances. Thanks to its high wings and efficient flaps, the aircraft can generate maximum lift even at low speeds, enabling take-offs and landings on runways as short as 350 meters. This capability is further enhanced by its robust landing gear, capable of withstanding uneven surfaces such as beaches, glaciers or dirt runways.

One of the key features of the Twin Otter is its versatility. It can be configured to carry passengers, freight, or a combination of both, and is even capable of landing on water when fitted with floats. This flexibility makes it an ideal aircraft for humanitarian missions, medical evacuations, and scheduled services in remote areas. The Twin Otter is used by regional airlines, governments and non-governmental organizations worldwide.

The success of the DHC-6 lies not only in its performance, but also in its reliability. Capable of operating in extreme climatic conditions, from scorching deserts to the icy expanses of the Arctic, the Twin Otter has proven its robustness and ability to operate where other aircraft cannot. This makes it a preferred choice for missions in environments where safety margins are low and the ability to land and take off quickly is essential.

Today, more than 50 years after its introduction, the Twin Otter continues to fly in the remotest corners of the globe. Its heritage as an aircraft designed for short landings and its ability to operate in extreme conditions make it an enduring example of successful aeronautical engineering. The DHC-6 Twin Otter remains an aviation icon, proving that an aircraft's ability to adapt to harsh environments can be as crucial as the most advanced technology.

# Fact 40 - The commercial plane that flies at Mach 2

The commercial aircraft capable of flying at Mach 2, twice the speed of sound, is the famous Concorde. Developed jointly by France and the UK, this supersonic aircraft entered service in 1976, offering commercial flights at unprecedented speeds. Concorde could reach a cruising speed of 2,180 km/h (Mach 2.04), enabling passengers to cross the Atlantic in just over three hours, a performance that remains unmatched to this day in civil aviation.

Concorde was powered by four Rolls-Royce/Snecma Olympus 593 engines, specially designed for supersonic flight. These engines, derived from those used on military aircraft, incorporated an afterburner, or reheat system, which increased thrust by injecting additional fuel into the exhaust gases. This technology enabled Concorde to reach Mach 2 quickly after takeoff, while maintaining stable performance at high altitudes, generally 18,000 meters, where the air is thinner and friction is reduced.

Concorde's design was as revolutionary as its performance. With its slender fuselage and delta wings, the aircraft was optimized for high-speed flight. The aerodynamic shape of the delta wing, combined with the use of light but strong materials, minimized drag while maximizing lift at supersonic speeds. This design also contributed to the aircraft's exceptional manoeuvrability, particularly during the critical take-off and landing phases.

However, flying at Mach 2 was not without its challenges. The heat generated by air friction at these high speeds caused Concorde's fuselage to stretch by 15 to 30 centimetres during flight. Engineers had to take this phenomenon into account when designing the aircraft, using materials capable of withstanding temperatures of up to 127°C on the surface of the nose and wings. In addition, high operating costs and the intense noise generated as the Concorde passed through the sound barrier limited its access to certain roads and airports.

Concorde flew for 27 years, mainly linking New York to London and Paris, before being retired in 2003. Despite the end of its commercial operation, Concorde remains an aviation icon, representing the ambition and innovation of the aeronautical industry. Flying at Mach 2 aboard this legendary aircraft offered thousands of passengers a unique experience, transforming the journey into a true technological feat.

# Fact 41 - First aircraft with a pressurized cockpit

The first aircraft to be equipped with a pressurized cockpit was the Boeing 307 Stratoliner, a revolutionary aircraft introduced in 1938. Designed for commercial transport, the Stratoliner offered pilots and passengers a more comfortable flying experience at high altitudes, where air is too scarce to be breathed without assistance. This innovation took commercial aviation to a new level, making it possible to fly longer and faster above the clouds, at altitudes of up to 6,000 meters.

The Boeing 307 was based on the B-17 Flying Fortress bomber, but with an enlarged fuselage and, above all, a fully pressurized cabin. This pressurization system, a first in aviation history, made it possible to maintain a comfortable atmospheric pressure inside the aircraft, even when the outside reached altitudes where the air became too thin for human comfort. Thanks to this innovation, the Stratoliner could fly well above turbulence and adverse weather conditions, offering a more stable and enjoyable flight.

The Stratoliner's pressurized cockpit also improved pilot safety and performance. Before this innovation, pilots were forced to wear oxygen masks at high altitudes, which was uncomfortable and limited their efficiency over long distances. With a pressurized cockpit, pilots could work in an environment similar to that at sea level, reducing fatigue and the risks associated with hypoxia, a condition caused by a lack of oxygen.

The introduction of the Boeing 307 marked the beginning of a new era in commercial aviation, in which passenger comfort and the ability to fly at higher altitudes became priorities. Although only 10 examples of this model were built due to the interruption of production during the Second World War, the Stratoliner left a lasting legacy. Its pressurization system was quickly adopted by other aircraft, forever changing the way airliners are designed and operated.

Today, pressurization is standard on all commercial aircraft, enabling flight at altitudes where air is scarcer without compromising the comfort and safety of passengers and crew. The Boeing 307 Stratoliner is thus recognized not only for its contribution to commercial aviation, but also as a pioneer of technologies that make air travel safer and more enjoyable for millions of people around the world.

# Fact 42 - The airplane that can carry a tank

One of the most iconic aircraft for its ability to carry battle tanks is the Lockheed C-5 Galaxy, an American military transport aircraft introduced in 1970. Designed to meet the logistical needs of the armed forces, the C-5 Galaxy is capable of transporting heavy loads over long distances, including main battle tanks, helicopters and even disassembled aircraft. With a payload capacity of over 122 tonnes, this aircraft has revolutionized the way armies can rapidly deploy heavy forces around the world.

The C-5 Galaxy was designed to transport large quantities of military equipment quickly and efficiently, including tanks such as the M1 Abrams, which weighs around 60 tonnes. Thanks to its large cargo bay, accessible from both the front and rear of the aircraft, the C-5 can load and unload heavy vehicles directly onto and off ramps, facilitating complex logistical operations. This feature is crucial to military operations, where speed of deployment can mean the difference between success and failure.

The aircraft is equipped with four General Electric TF39 jet engines, giving it sufficient power to take off with maximum loads even from relatively short runways. Once airborne, the C-5 Galaxy can cover intercontinental distances non-stop, enabling armored forces to be moved rapidly from one theater of operations to another. Its ability to transport tanks and other heavy vehicles over long distances makes it an essential strategic asset for US armed forces and their allies.

The C-5 Galaxy is impressive not only for its size and load capacity, but also for its versatility. In addition to carrying tanks, it can also serve as a flying hospital, a mobile command center, or even a temporary air base. This flexibility has been demonstrated time and again during conflicts and humanitarian missions, where the C-5 has played a crucial role in the rapid delivery of equipment and personnel to remote or hard-to-reach areas.

Today, the C-5 Galaxy continues to serve with the US Air Force, although it has been modernized with new engines and improved navigation systems. Its ability to transport tanks and other heavy loads over vast distances remains unsurpassed, making this aircraft a central element of modern military logistics. The C-5 symbolizes the power of aeronautical engineering in the service of military operations, demonstrating that aviation can play a decisive role in force projection and rapid reaction on the battlefield.

# Fact 43 - The longest non-stop flight

The longest non-stop flight ever made by a commercial aircraft was accomplished by a Boeing 777-200LR operated by Qatar Airways in 2005. This record-breaking flight linked Hong Kong to London, but followed a route that crossed the Pacific Ocean, North America and the Atlantic Ocean, covering a distance of 21,601 kilometers in 22 hours and 42 minutes. This flight, designed to demonstrate the capabilities of the Boeing 777-200LR, exceeded all expectations and remains a feat of endurance for commercial aviation.

The Boeing 777-200LR, nicknamed the "Worldliner", has been specially designed for ultra-long-haul flights. This model is equipped with additional fuel tanks, enabling it to carry up to 181,000 liters of fuel - almost twice the capacity of a medium-haul aircraft. This extraordinary range enables the 777-200LR to fly non-stop to virtually any point on the globe, making direct connections possible between cities on opposite sides of the world.

For this record-breaking flight, Qatar Airways chose an unusual route, longer than necessary to maximize the distance covered. The aircraft took off from Hong Kong and flew eastwards over the Pacific, Alaska, Canada and the North Atlantic before landing at London Heathrow. The aim of the trip was to test the aircraft's limits and demonstrate its ability to operate in a variety of conditions, including high-altitude flight and extreme temperature changes.

During this flight, the aircraft carried a team of pilots, engineers and crew members who took turns throughout the journey to ensure a safe and efficient flight. The Boeing 777-200LR was also optimized for passenger comfort, with a cabin specially fitted out for this exceptional flight. Despite the length of the journey, the aircraft maintained efficient fuel consumption and completed the flight with sufficient reserves, proving the reliability of its design for extremely long flights.

This record-breaking flight not only showcased the impressive capabilities of the Boeing 777-200LR, it also marked a turning point in commercial aviation, paving the way for a new era of ultra-long-haul flights. Thanks to this technology, routes that once seemed impossible are now a reality, connecting continents more directly and faster than ever before. The Hong Kong-London flight remains a benchmark of endurance and technology in aviation history.

# Fact 44 - The plane that broke the altitude record

The aircraft that holds the absolute altitude record for a manned flight is the Lockheed SR-71 Blackbird. This strategic reconnaissance aircraft, designed to fly at extreme speeds and altitudes, reached an impressive 25,929 meters (85,069 feet) on July 28, 1976. This record was set by American pilot William J. "Bill" Fox during a test flight over Beale Air Force Base, California, cementing the SR-71's reputation as one of the most advanced aircraft of its time.

The SR-71 Blackbird was developed in the 1960s by Lockheed's Skunk Works division, headed by legendary engineer Clarence "Kelly" Johnson. Designed for high-altitude reconnaissance missions, the aircraft had to be able to fly higher and faster than any threat, including surface-to-air missiles. With a top speed of over Mach 3 (approx. 3,540 km/h), the SR-71 could not only evade radar detection but also interception, thanks to its ability to climb rapidly to altitudes where no other aircraft could follow.

The SR-71's record altitude was made possible by its Pratt & Whitney J58 engines, which are capable of operating optimally at very high altitudes. These jet engines, combined with a unique aerodynamic design and heat-resistant materials, enabled the aircraft to maintain stable performance even in the rarefied atmosphere of the upper stratosphere. The Blackbird was also equipped with advanced survival systems for its pilots, enabling them to withstand the extreme conditions of flight at very high altitudes.

The SR-71's altitude record has never been officially beaten by any other manned aircraft, although some unmanned experimental aircraft have been able to reach higher altitudes. The SR-71 operated until its retirement in 1998, carrying out strategic reconnaissance missions around the world. Its unique design, exceptional speed and ability to fly at record altitudes made it a true symbol of the technological superiority of the air at the time.

The Lockheed SR-71 Blackbird remains an aviation icon, admired for its unrivalled performance and crucial role in intelligence gathering during the Cold War. The altitude record it set in 1976 is a testament to the ingenuity and vision that pushed back the boundaries of what aviation could achieve, paving the way for new explorations in the skies and beyond.

# Fact 45 - First aircraft to take off from a carrier

The first aircraft to take off from a carrier was a Eugene Ely, on November 14, 1910. This aviation pioneer made history with a daring exploit from the USS Birmingham, a U.S. Navy cruiser stationed in Virginia's Chesapeake Bay. The aircraft used for this historic flight was a Curtiss Model D, a fragile biplane powered by a 50-horsepower engine, very different from powerful modern aircraft.

Eugene Ely, a civilian aviator recruited by the navy for this test, already had a reputation for aerial prowess. For the flight, a 24-meter wooden platform had been specially built on the ship's foredeck. Ely took off in the late afternoon, despite uncertain weather conditions and widespread skepticism. The biplane sped down the short runway before plunging slightly into the sea, the wheels briefly touching the water before the aircraft regained altitude. This successful take-off proved that aircraft could operate from ships at sea, a revolutionary idea at the time.

This first takeoff from an aircraft carrier was not only a technical feat, but also a demonstration of future possibilities for the projection of air power at sea. After this success, Ely continued to work with the navy, and two months later he carried out the first landing on a ship, this time on the USS Pennsylvania, demonstrating that aircraft could not only take off, but also return safely to land on a ship at sea.

The Curtiss Model D used for this mission was a simple aircraft, built mainly of wood and canvas, with a structure that was light but strong enough to withstand the stresses of taking off from an offshore platform. This flight demonstrated the importance of adapting aircraft for naval operations, and paved the way for the development of the first dedicated aircraft carriers, which were to become essential elements of navies worldwide over the following decades.

Today, aircraft carriers are symbols of military power, and air operations at sea have become routine for navies worldwide. Eugene Ely's exploit in 1910 has gone down in history as the moment when naval aviation really took off, forever transforming naval warfare and military strategies.

# Fact 46 - The hovering aircraft

One of the aircraft most notable for its ability to hover is the Harrier Jump Jet. Designed by the British company Hawker Siddeley in the 1960s, this revolutionary aircraft is able to take off and land vertically, as well as maintain a hover, a capability usually found in helicopters but rarely in jets. The Harrier made aviation history as the first jet to possess this capability, changing the face of military operations.

The secret behind this feat lies in its vectored thrust engines. The Harrier is powered by a Rolls-Royce Pegasus engine, whose thrust can be directed downwards by means of steerable nozzles. These nozzles enable the Harrier to generate the lift required for vertical take-off, and then hover or transition to conventional horizontal flight. This flexibility makes the Harrier ideal for operations in restricted environments, such as aircraft carrier decks or forward bases where conventional runways are unavailable or impractical.

The Harrier has been used successfully by a number of armed forces, notably during the Falklands War in 1982, when it proved its worth by providing air cover for British forces in a remote theater of operations. Its ability to take off and land on small aircraft carriers, as well as its ability to hover for attack or reconnaissance missions, made it an indispensable asset in situations where flexibility and speed of intervention were essential.

This ability to hover gives the Harrier a significant tactical advantage. For example, it can remain in position to observe or attack a target without having to circle around it, as is the case with traditional fixed-wing aircraft. This enables it to react more quickly to developments on the battlefield, offering air superiority in situations where speed and precision are crucial.

The Harrier Jump Jet paved the way for other vertical take-off and landing (VTOL) aircraft, such as the F-35B Lightning II. However, it remains an emblematic example of aeronautical innovation, having transformed military air operations through its unique ability to combine the power of a fighter jet with the maneuverability of a helicopter. The Harrier's legacy lives on in modern aviation, where versatility and the ability to operate in difficult conditions continue to be priorities for aircraft designers.

# Fact 47 - First commercial jet flight

The first commercial jet flight took place on May 2, 1952, marking the beginning of a new era in air transport. This historic event was accomplished by a de Havilland Comet, a revolutionary British aircraft designed to exploit the superior performance of jet engines. The flight, operated by British Overseas Airways Corporation (BOAC), flew from London to Johannesburg, South Africa, with several stopovers en route.

The de Havilland Comet was the first airliner to be equipped with jet engines, a technology that offered much higher speeds and cruising altitudes than the propeller-driven aircraft of the day. The Rolls-Royce Ghost engines, mounted in the Comet's wings, enabled the aircraft to fly at a cruising speed of 800 km/h and an altitude of 12,000 meters, above most turbulence and adverse weather conditions, offering a faster and more comfortable flight for passengers.

The inaugural flight of the Comet marked a turning point in commercial aviation. For the first time, passengers could cross long distances in a much shorter time, taking advantage of the pressurized cabin and the aircraft's characteristic large windows, which offered an unobstructed view of the landscape below. This flight not only demonstrated the commercial viability of jet aircraft, it also laid the foundations for what was to become a standard in the airline industry.

However, the Comet also encountered significant challenges. Shortly after its introduction, several accidents revealed structural weaknesses due to material fatigue, caused by the repeated pressures of high-altitude flight. These incidents led to the temporary suspension of Comet flights and a thorough investigation that uncovered critical problems in the design. Despite these setbacks, the lessons learned from Comet have led to significant improvements in jet safety.

Today, the legacy of the de Havilland Comet lives on in every modern jet. Although its early years were marked by challenges, the Comet paved the way for the fast, efficient air transport we know today. It remains an aviation icon, not only for being the first to introduce jets to commercial transport, but also for forever transforming the way the world travels.

# Fact 48 - The plane that carries space shuttles

The aircraft designed to carry NASA's space shuttles is the Boeing 747 Shuttle Carrier Aircraft (SCA). This unique model of the famous Boeing 747 was modified to perform the impressive task of carrying space shuttles such as Enterprise, Atlantis and Endeavour on its back. This airlifter played a crucial role in the U.S. space program, moving shuttles between manufacturing facilities, landing sites and launch centers.

The Boeing 747 SCA was fitted with special fuselage attachments to secure the space shuttle to its back. These modifications also included strengthening the aircraft's structure and adding vertical stabilizers on the tail to compensate for the aerodynamic disturbances caused by the shuttle. When carrying a shuttle, the 747 SCA resembled a giant of the air, with an imposing mass on its back, defying the laws of physics.

One of the most spectacular flights of the Boeing 747 SCA took place in 1983, when the aircraft carried the shuttle Challenger from NASA's Florida launch pad to the Johnson Space Center in Texas. This type of mission was essential for the shuttles, particularly after their return to Earth, where they sometimes had to be transported back to their point of departure for another mission or for repairs. The 747 SCA thus enabled NASA to maintain the logistical flexibility vital to the success of space missions.

The 747 SCA was not only used for transport missions. It was also used in demonstration flights, allowing the public to see the Space Shuttle up close as it was transported between different sites across the USA. These flights helped inspire an entire generation of aerospace enthusiasts, offering a tangible glimpse of how aviation and space exploration could be integrated.

Today, Boeing 747 SCAs have been retired from service with the end of the Space Shuttle program in 2011, but they remain on display in museums as symbols of the ingenuity and collaboration between aeronautics and space exploration. These special aircraft are a visual reminder of the days when space shuttles ruled the skies, carried by planes that seemed almost as legendary as the missions they supported.

# Fact 49 - First plane to fly above the clouds

The first aircraft to fly above the clouds was the Bleriot XI, piloted by Louis Blériot himself, in 1910. This feat marked a milestone in aviation history, demonstrating the ability of aircraft to reach previously unexplored altitudes. At the time, flying above the clouds was not only a technical feat, but also an unprecedented visual experience, where the pilot suddenly found himself in a bright, clear world, far removed from the sometimes harsh weather conditions below.

Louis Blériot, famous for being the first to fly across the English Channel in 1909, was an aviation pioneer constantly seeking new challenges. The Bleriot XI, a wood-and-canvas monoplane with a 25-horsepower engine, was a relatively simple aircraft, but Blériot had modified his plane to make it lighter and more efficient, enabling it to climb to altitudes where few other planes could venture at the time.

Climbing above the clouds was more than just a challenge of height. It symbolized aviation's ambition to conquer the skies, offering pilots a new perspective on the world. In those days, flight instruments were rudimentary, and pilots had to rely on their eyesight to navigate. Flying above the clouds meant entering unknown territory, where the horizon disappeared, and only the blue sky surrounded the plane, creating a sensation of freedom and isolation.

This feat opened up new possibilities for aviation. Flying above the clouds meant avoiding turbulence and bad weather, making flights safer and more comfortable. This breakthrough also helped improve navigation techniques and on-board instruments, as pilots needed new tools to find their way in these unprecedented conditions.

Louis Blériot's flight above the clouds has gone down in aviation history as a demonstration of the courage and innovation that characterized the early years of aviation. It inspired other aviators to push the limits of what was possible even further, helping to make aviation a reliable and efficient means of transport in the decades that followed.

# Fact 50 - The airplane designed to withstand storms

One of the most remarkable aircraft designed to withstand storms is the Lockheed WC-130 Hercules, a weather reconnaissance aircraft used by the US Air Force. This model, derived from the famous C-130 Hercules, is specifically equipped to penetrate the heart of storms, including hurricanes, to gather crucial data on their intensity and trajectory. Dubbed "hurricane hunters", these aircraft are designed to cope with extreme weather conditions that few other aircraft could endure.

The WC-130 is reinforced to withstand the high winds, heavy rain and extreme turbulence encountered at the center of storms. It is equipped with sophisticated measuring instruments, including Doppler radars, pressure and temperature sensors, as well as devices for dropping probes into the storm. These instruments collect data in real time, which is essential for meteorologists to predict storm evolution and issue accurate warnings, thus protecting lives and property.

The mission of the "hurricane hunters" is both dangerous and vital. WC-130 crews must fly directly through the eyewall of the storm, where conditions are at their most violent, to obtain accurate measurements. They often fly at low altitude, just a few thousand feet above the raging sea, amid winds that can exceed 200 km/h. This ability to operate in such extreme conditions makes the WC-130 a unique aircraft, designed not only to survive the storm, but also to unravel its mysteries.

In addition to its robustness, the WC-130 is designed to be modular and adaptable. It can be rapidly configured for a variety of meteorological missions, whether tracking a hurricane or monitoring a snowstorm. This operational flexibility is essential for meteorological agencies that need to be ready to respond to a wide variety of hazardous weather scenarios.

The Lockheed WC-130 Hercules has played a crucial role in modern meteorology, providing a better understanding of extreme weather phenomena and contributing to public safety. These aircraft, and the courageous crews who fly them, are at the heart of forecasting and preparing for the most powerful storms nature can produce, making this aircraft a true unsung hero of aviation.

# Fact 51 - The world's smallest helicopter

The world's smallest helicopter is the GEN H-4, designed by Japanese engineer Gennai Yanagisawa. This ultra-compact helicopter, which weighs just 70 kg, was developed in 2000 and is small enough to be carried by a single person. With its minimalist design, the GEN H-4 is powered by two piston engines of 10 hp each, driving two counter-rotating rotors, eliminating the need for a tail rotor.

This tiny helicopter can fly at a maximum speed of 90 km/h and can reach an altitude of 3,000 meters. Despite its small size, the GEN H-4 is surprisingly stable and maneuverable, making it a remarkable technological feat in the field of personal aviation. It is designed to be easily flown, even by those without extensive aviation training, thanks to its simple, intuitive control system.

The GEN H-4 was originally conceived as a leisure machine, offering aviation enthusiasts a unique experience of personal helicopter flight. Its designer, Yanagisawa, wanted to create a helicopter accessible to all, with the idea that everyone could one day own their own helicopter, just as one owns a car. Although not mass-produced, the GEN H-4 remains a fascinating example of innovation in the field of light helicopters.

The helicopter attracted a great deal of international interest when it was unveiled, due to its small size and unusual design. It was shown at various air shows, where it impressed with its ability to fly stably yet extremely lightly. It also became a popular subject among aviation enthusiasts and engineers, fascinated by the idea of being able to design ever smaller and more efficient helicopters.

To this day, the GEN H-4 remains the smallest operational helicopter ever built, and embodies aviation's quest to push back the boundaries of what's possible, combining simplicity and efficiency in an aircraft that defies expectations. This micro-helicopter is not only a technical curiosity, but also an inspiration for the future of light and personal aviation.

# Fact 52 - First flight by a child pilot

The first child-piloted flight in aviation history dates back to July 10, 1927, when Elinor Smith, a young girl of just 16, took the controls of a Waco 9 biplane. Elinor Smith was not only passionate about aviation, she already had significant experience as a co-pilot with seasoned aviators. But on that day, she became one of the youngest pilots to fly solo, marking an incredible achievement in a still very new field.

Born in 1911, Elinor Smith was fascinated by airplanes from an early age. At a time when aviation was still largely dominated by men, she persevered with her dream of becoming a pilot. Encouraged by her parents, she began taking flying lessons at the age of 10. This flight in 1927 was not her first contact with an airplane, but it was the first time she had flown alone, demonstrating impressive courage and mastery for her age.

The flight took place in New York State, where Elinor took off from a small local airfield. The Waco 9, a biplane used mainly for training, was a robust but demanding aircraft to fly. Elinor handled the aircraft with such skill that her flight was widely acclaimed by observers. The flight was not only an achievement for her, but also a symbol of the ability of young people to achieve extraordinary things when they are passionate and well trained.

After this flight, Elinor Smith continued to break barriers in the world of aviation. She became a renowned test pilot, setting several speed, altitude and endurance records during her career. Her feat in 1927 is often regarded as one of the first proofs that aviation was not just a matter for experienced adults, but could also be accessible to talented young pilots.

Elinor Smith's story remains a source of inspiration for many young aviation enthusiasts. Her first solo flight, at just 16 years of age, showed that age need not be a barrier to achieving great things, especially when driven by true passion. Elinor paved the way for other young pilots, proving that childhood dreams can literally take flight.

# Fact 53 - The plane with the most engines

The aircraft with the most engines ever built is the Kalinin K-7, an experimental Soviet aircraft designed in the 1930s by engineer Konstantin Kalinin. This colossal aircraft was equipped with no fewer than seven engines, a rare configuration even at a time when the limits of aerodynamics were constantly being pushed back. Six of these engines were mounted on the wings, and a seventh was placed at the rear of the fuselage, providing the thrust needed to power this enormous aircraft.

The Kalinin K-7 had a wingspan of 53 meters and weighed around 24 tons empty. It was designed for large-scale transport missions, capable of carrying over 100 passengers or 16 tons of freight. Despite its size and weight, the aircraft's seven engines enabled it to reach a top speed of 225 km/h, an impressive performance for the time. The aircraft also boasted a vast interior, designed to accommodate passengers in relative comfort - an innovative ambition for a military aircraft of this size.

The K-7 represented a bold advance in aircraft design, but was never put into large-scale production due to a number of technical problems. On its maiden flight in 1933, the K-7 showed signs of excessive vibration, a problem that proved difficult to resolve. In addition, the aircraft was involved in an accident during a subsequent test flight, leading to the abandonment of the project. Despite this, the Kalinin K-7 left an indelible mark on aviation history as a multi-engine aircraft, a concept that has never been equalled in terms of the number of engines.

The idea of using so many engines on a single aircraft was motivated by the need for power to take off and fly such a massive aircraft. At the time, aircraft engines were not as powerful as they are today, so the solution was to multiply the number of engines to spread the load. Although this approach didn't lead to commercial success, it did contribute to the evolution of large-scale aviation concepts, inspiring engineers to explore new solutions to the challenges of propulsion and stability.

Today, the Kalinin K-7 is often cited as one of the most ambitious and unusual aviation projects ever attempted. Its legacy is one of innovation, experimentation and a willingness to go beyond conventional limits, even if this meant taking considerable risks. The aircraft, with its seven engines, remains a symbol of the ingenuity and courage of aviation pioneers.

# Fact 54 - First transcontinental passenger flight

The first transcontinental passenger flight in history took place in 1929, linking New York to Los Angeles. This epic crossing, operated by Transcontinental Air Transport (TAT), marked a decisive turning point in air transport, offering passengers a fast alternative to long train journeys across the USA. The flight, which took almost 48 hours, included segments by plane combined with overnight train journeys, an innovative solution for the time.

The journey began in New York, where passengers boarded a Ford Trimotor, a sturdy three-engine plane capable of carrying up to 12 passengers. This aircraft, nicknamed "the Tin Goose" because of its metal hull, offered a relatively high level of comfort for the time, with leather seats and windows for admiring the scenery. The first leg of the flight took passengers to Columbus, Ohio, where they took a train for the night before returning to the plane the following day.

The idea behind this service was to considerably reduce travel time between the two American coasts. At the time, crossing the country by train took more than three days. With this combined plane-train service, TAT managed to cut this time in half. Although the route included several stopovers, notably in Waynoka, Kansas, and Clovis, New Mexico, it represented a logistical and technological feat for the time.

Passengers on this first transcontinental flight were not only aviation pioneers, they were also among the first to experience long-distance commercial air service. The flight offered a glimpse into the future of air transport, demonstrating that it was possible to rapidly link destinations thousands of kilometers apart. Although rudimentary by modern standards, this service laid the foundations for intercontinental air transport as we know it today.

This first transcontinental passenger flight was a veritable revolution in commercial aviation. It paved the way for ever longer and more complex air travel, culminating in the advent of direct non-stop flights that today enable people to travel the globe in just a few hours. The story of this flight remains an important milestone, showing how aviation transformed the world by bringing together continents once separated by days of travel.

# Fact 55 - The plane that flew the lowest

One of the lowest flights ever recorded was performed by American pilot Jimmy Doolittle during a flight demonstration in 1929. In this spectacular maneuver, Doolittle piloted a Curtiss R3C-2 at an incredibly low altitude, flying over the surface of a lake just a few meters above the water. This feat demonstrated not only his extraordinary skill as a pilot, but also the aircraft's capabilities, which he mastered with frightening precision.

The Curtiss R3C-2 was a racing seaplane, designed specifically for competitions where speed and agility were essential. Doolittle, already a world-renowned pilot, was used to pushing the limits of what was thought possible in flight. Flying at such a low altitude, he had to maintain absolute control of the aircraft to avoid any potentially fatal contact with the water's surface. The slightest error in calculation or piloting could have had dramatic consequences.

This demonstration took place as part of the Schneider Trophy, a prestigious aeronautical competition that challenged pilots to fly at breakneck speeds while maintaining impeccable technical control. Doolittle's low-flying performance not only impressed spectators, but also highlighted the extreme risks pilots took to achieve victory. This competition was a veritable stage for the greatest aeronautical feats of the era.

Flying at very low altitude presents unique challenges. At this height, turbulence is much stronger, and the slightest ripple or irregularity in the terrain can spell disaster. Pilots like Doolittle needed superhuman reflexes and intense concentration to maintain the exact altitude required. Today, this type of flying is highly regulated due to the dangers it presents, but at the time, it represented one of the purest forms of the art of piloting.

Jimmy Doolittle's incredibly low flight has gone down in aviation history as one of the most daring pilots of his time. His demonstration of courage and precision not only left a lasting impression, but also laid the foundations for future feats in aviation, where altitude control becomes crucial in critical situations. This event is a perfect example of how aviation has always been a field where innovation and courage meet at sometimes very low altitudes.

# Fact 56 - First airplane designed for scientific research

The first aircraft designed specifically for scientific research was the Lockheed U-2, developed in the 1950s. Initially designed for high-altitude reconnaissance, the U-2 was quickly adapted to carry out scientific missions, notably in meteorology and atmospheric studies. Its ability to fly at altitudes of over 21,000 meters, well above commercial aircraft and most atmospheric turbulence, made it an ideal tool for collecting precise, unprecedented data.

From its very first flights, the U-2 revolutionized the way scientists could observe and understand the Earth's atmosphere. The aircraft was equipped with instruments capable of measuring the chemical composition of the air, detecting radioactive particles, and taking high-resolution photographs of the Earth's surface. These capabilities were particularly useful during the Cold War, when scientists used the data collected by the U-2 to monitor nuclear tests and better understand the dispersion of radiation in the atmosphere.

One of the U-2's most famous scientific missions took place in 1962, when the plane flew over the Pacific Ocean to study a powerful hurricane. Flying at an altitude unattainable for other aircraft, the U-2 was able to collect crucial meteorological data that helped improve storm forecasting models. These missions demonstrated the incredible potential of aircraft as research platforms, capable of exploring otherwise inaccessible environments.

Over the decades, the U-2 continued to be used for scientific missions, evolving with technological advances. The aircraft was equipped with increasingly sophisticated sensors, capable of measuring everything from greenhouse gases to changes in the ozone layer. Its role in scientific research has led to a better understanding of global climate processes and the monitoring of large-scale environmental changes.

The Lockheed U-2 remains a symbol of the intersection between aviation and science. Originally designed for military missions, it demonstrated that aircraft could play a key role in scientific research, offering a unique perspective on our planet. Its legacy lives on, as it continues to inspire the development of new aircraft and drones designed to explore and monitor our world in ever more precise and sophisticated ways.

# Fact 57 - First plane to fly on wind power

The first aircraft to harness wind power for flight was the Windflier, an innovative prototype designed in the 1980s by a group of researchers specializing in renewable energies. This ambitious project aimed to demonstrate that it was possible to use wind power to propel an aircraft, by exploiting a rotor technology capable of capturing air currents at high altitude and converting them into mechanical energy.

The Windflier was equipped with a large propeller at the front of the aircraft, connected to an electric generator. This generator transformed the wind's kinetic energy into electricity, powering the electric motors that propelled the aircraft. Although innovative, this concept posed a number of technical challenges. In particular, it had to be guaranteed that the airplane could maintain a constant speed while capturing enough energy to power its motors.

In its first flight tests, the Windflier was able to maintain stable flight using only the energy captured by its rotor. This represented a significant breakthrough in ecological aviation, long before environmental concerns became central to the aeronautical industry. The aircraft demonstrated that wind, an abundant and renewable resource, could be used as an energy source for aviation, opening up new possibilities for sustainable air transport.

However, the Windflier was never commercialized due to technological limitations at the time. The equipment needed to capture and convert wind energy was still too heavy and cumbersome for practical use in a commercial aircraft. Despite this, the Windflier remains a pioneering project, illustrating the creativity and ingenuity of engineers seeking to push back the boundaries of what is possible in aviation.

Today, although wind-powered aviation is not yet a mainstream reality, the ideas and concepts explored by the Windflier continue to inspire research into renewable energies and alternative propulsion technologies. This project is a reminder that innovation in aviation has always been driven by the desire to discover new, more efficient and environmentally-friendly ways of flying.

# Fact 58 - First fully automated flight

The first fully automated flight, without direct human intervention, was achieved in 1984 by an experimental aircraft called the Autonomous Aircraft System (AAS). This innovative project was developed by NASA in collaboration with several research institutes to demonstrate that aircraft could not only take off and land without a pilot, but also navigate safely following a predefined flight plan.

The aircraft used for this experiment was a small model equipped with multiple sensors, a satellite navigation system (GPS), and an on-board computer capable of making decisions in real time. The latter analyzed the data provided by the sensors to adjust the plane's trajectory, manage speed, and even avoid potential obstacles. This technology represented a major breakthrough in flight automation.

During the flight, the computer took charge of every stage of the flight, from taxiing to landing. This success proved that an aircraft could be controlled entirely by computer systems, without human intervention, opening up fascinating prospects for the future of aviation, particularly in terms of safety and efficiency. Automation not only reduced human error, but also optimized fuel consumption and minimized flight times.

This historic flight marked the beginning of a new era in aviation, with automated systems becoming increasingly sophisticated and commonplace in commercial aviation. Today, although pilots still play a crucial role, most modern airliners use autopilot systems for the majority of the flight. These systems, which have their roots in projects such as AAS, are capable of handling complex situations and reacting rapidly to changing conditions.

The AAS experience also laid the foundations for the development of drones and unmanned aircraft, which are now used in a multitude of fields, from military operations to rescue missions and environmental monitoring. This first fully automated flight demonstrated that aviation can evolve beyond human limits, integrating technologies that make flying safer, more efficient and more accessible.

# Fact 59 - The plane with the propellers turning in the wrong direction

Among the most fascinating innovations in aviation, counter-rotating propellers - i.e. propellers turning in opposite directions on the same engine - occupy a unique place. One of the most emblematic examples of this technology is the Soviet Tupolev Tu-95 strategic bomber designed in the 1950s. This type of propeller offers distinct advantages, including greater aerodynamic efficiency and reduced reaction torque, which tends to turn the aircraft in the opposite direction to the propellers.

The Tu-95 is powered by four turboprop engines, each equipped with two counter-rotating propellers. This configuration maximizes power while reducing drag, resulting in higher speed and more efficient fuel consumption. For an aircraft of its size, this design is particularly effective for maintaining long missions at high altitude and over long distances.

The counter-rotating propeller design is ingenious: the two sets of propellers rotate in opposite directions, cancelling out the torque that could destabilize the aircraft. This also results in a more even distribution of thrust, enhancing in-flight stability. What's more, this configuration recovers some of the energy lost in the wake of the first propeller, increasing the engine's overall efficiency.

The use of these propellers on the Tu-95 enabled this aircraft to become one of the fastest propeller-driven bombers ever built, capable of flying at speeds approaching those of early jets. This bomber is still in service today, a testament to the durability and efficiency of this technology. The distinctive noise produced by its counter-rotating propellers even earned it the nickname "Bear" among NATO forces.

This technology is not commonplace due to its complexity and higher maintenance costs, but it remains a fascinating example of aeronautical ingenuity. Counter-rotating propellers show how a specific innovation can dramatically improve an aircraft's performance, maximizing fuel efficiency while delivering exceptional power, making the Tu-95 a legendary aircraft in aviation history.

# Fact 60 - First plane to cross the equator

The first flight to cross the equator marked a milestone in aviation history, demonstrating the ability of aircraft to cover long distances and cross natural boundaries. This feat was achieved in 1924 by the "Chicago" aircraft, a Douglas World Cruiser, on an expedition organized by the US Army Air Service to complete the first aerial circumnavigation of the globe.

The "Chicago" aircraft, piloted by Lieutenant Lowell H. Smith, was one of four specially modified for this 44,000-kilometer mission. On May 6, 1924, the crew crossed the equator over the Atlantic Ocean, between the Cape Verde Islands and South America. This symbolic crossing was a crucial milestone in their journey, illustrating the ability of aircraft to cross hemispheres and overcome previously insurmountable geographical challenges.

The weather conditions and unpredictable climate of the equatorial region presented considerable challenges for the aviators. Despite tropical storms and mechanical hazards, the crew of the "Chicago" managed to stay on course, demonstrating the endurance of the aircraft and the determination of the pilots of the time.

Crossing the equator was not only a technical feat, but also a symbolic achievement that proved aviation could unite the two hemispheres. It also reinforced the credibility of aircraft as a reliable means of long-distance transport, paving the way for the expansion of international air routes.

The expedition was successfully completed in September 1924, making the "Chicago" and its crew pioneers of world aviation. The crossing of the equator remains a defining moment of this adventure, underlining the conquest of the skies and the expansion of aviation horizons. This flight inspired generations of pilots and engineers to push back even further the limits of what is possible in aviation.

# Fact 61 - First aircraft designed for underwater surveillance

Aviation has always evolved to meet specific military and civilian needs, and one of the most intriguing developments has been the design of aircraft for underwater surveillance. The first aircraft specifically designed for this mission was the Lockheed P-3 Orion, introduced in the 1960s, which played a crucial role in the Cold War by detecting enemy submarines.

The P-3 Orion is a long-range maritime patrol aircraft equipped with sophisticated acoustic and electronic detection systems. It uses submerged sonar and sonobuoys to locate and track submarines below the water's surface. These capabilities enabled naval forces to monitor the movements of submarines, particularly those equipped with nuclear missiles, which was crucial to maintaining the strategic balance during the Cold War.

The aircraft has been designed to remain airborne for long periods, covering vast expanses of ocean. It can fly at low altitude for hours at a time, an essential asset for accurate, continuous detection of underwater targets. This endurance, combined with its ability to cover immense distances, makes it an indispensable tool for maritime surveillance and anti-submarine warfare.

In addition to its underwater surveillance missions, the P-3 Orion has also been used for general maritime reconnaissance, sea rescue and fisheries surveillance. This versatility has made it an aircraft widely used by air and sea forces around the world, and it remains in active service in many countries.

The development of the Lockheed P-3 Orion marked a turning point in military aviation, demonstrating how an aircraft could play a central role in maritime defense strategy. Its ability to detect and monitor underwater threats not only enhanced the security of nations, but also paved the way for future innovations in the design of specialized surveillance aircraft.

# Fact 62 - First double-fuselage aircraft

One of the most unique and daring concepts in aviation history is undoubtedly the twin-fuselage aircraft. The first such aircraft was the P-82 Twin Mustang, an American fighter developed at the end of the Second World War. This design, as impressive as it was unusual, was intended to improve fighter performance and endurance.

The P-82 Twin Mustang was designed by North American Aviation using two fuselages from the P-51 Mustang, one of the most famous fighters of its day. By linking these two fuselages by a central wing, engineers created an aircraft capable of long combat missions with great autonomy, ideal for long-range bomber escort missions. The idea behind this design was to enable the aircraft to stay airborne for longer, while still being able to carry two pilots, which was crucial for long missions.

This unique design also offered redundancy in terms of propulsion, since each fuselage had its own engine. This meant that even in the event of engine failure, the aircraft could still be flown and returned safely to base, increasing crew survival. In addition, this configuration enabled heavier armament and greater stability in flight, making it a formidable fighter.

Although the P-82 Twin Mustang was designed too late to take part in the Second World War, it played an important role in the early years of the Cold War, particularly during the Korean War. It became one of the first jet fighters to enter active service, illustrating how innovation in aeronautical design could push the boundaries of what was possible in military aviation.

The legacy of the P-82 Twin Mustang remains in the annals of aviation as a bold example of engineering, demonstrating that creativity and innovation can result in unique solutions to technological and strategic challenges. This model paved the way for other innovative concepts in aeronautics, inspiring engineers to think beyond established conventions.

# Fact 63 - The rocket-launching aircraft

The idea of an airplane launching a rocket sounds like something out of a science fiction story, but it was made possible by the revolutionary concept of the North American X-15. This rocket plane, developed in the 1950s, played a crucial role in space exploration and high-altitude experimentation. This program, led by NASA in collaboration with the US Air Force and the US Navy, broke new ground in aviation and astronautics.

The X-15 was designed to be carried under the wing of a modified B-52 bomber, known as a "mothership". Once aloft, the rocket plane was jettisoned and its liquid-propelled rocket engine ignited, propelling the X-15 to incredible speeds and altitudes. With suborbital flight capability, this aircraft was able to reach supersonic speeds and penetrate the limits of space, setting speed and altitude records that were not beaten until many years later.

What made the X-15 even more impressive was its ability to test technologies crucial to future space missions. In addition to its role in the study of high-speed aerodynamics, the aircraft also served as a platform for testing spacesuits, navigation systems and materials resistant to extreme temperatures, all of which were used in later space programs, including the Apollo missions.

The X-15 was used for small rocket launches and payload tests in the upper atmosphere. These experiments deepened our understanding of flight conditions at the frontier of space. The aircraft contributed directly to the technological advances that made manned spaceflight possible, marking an essential step between conventional aviation and spaceflight.

This program left a lasting legacy in aeronautics and space exploration, demonstrating that innovation and collaboration between the aviation and space industries can lead to extraordinary breakthroughs. The X-15 remains an icon of that era, symbolizing the pioneering spirit that pushed the limits of what was possible in the skies and beyond.

# Fact 64 - First flight over Antarctica

The first flight over Antarctica was a daring feat achieved by American explorer Richard E. Byrd in 1929. Aboard a three-engine Ford, the Floyd Bennett, Byrd and his crew took off from the base on Whale Bay to fly over the mysterious icy continent. This flight marked a crucial step in the exploration of this inhospitable and, at the time, barely-known region.

Flying conditions were extreme, with freezing temperatures and strong winds. The crew had to navigate across a totally white landscape, where visual cues were almost non-existent. Despite these challenges, Byrd and his crew managed to reach the South Pole, becoming the first to fly over it. This mission symbolized the spirit of adventure and innovation that characterized the golden age of aviation.

The aircraft used for this expedition was specially equipped to withstand the rigors of the Antarctic climate. The engines were protected against freezing, and the plane was loaded with provisions to enable the crew to survive in case of emergency. The success of this flight demonstrated not only the capabilities of aviation at the time, but also human ingenuity in the face of adversity.

This historic flight provided invaluable data on Antarctica, contributing to a better understanding of this mysterious continent. Byrd, already famous for his Arctic explorations, became an emblematic figure of polar exploration, and his feat continued to inspire future generations of explorers and aviators.

Richard E. Byrd's exploit has gone down in history as a decisive moment in Antarctic exploration. This daring flight not only paved the way for future scientific missions, but also proved that man could overcome the most extreme challenges through ingenuity, determination and daring.

# Fact 65 - The aircraft designed for rescue missions

Among aircraft specially designed for rescue missions, the Lockheed C-130 Hercules occupies a prime position. Initially designed as a military transport aircraft, the C-130 has proved exceptionally versatile, capable of operating in hostile environments and carrying out rescue missions in the most difficult conditions. Its rugged design, ability to land on short, unprepared runways, and long range have made it a preferred choice for rescue operations.

The C-130 has been used in a multitude of rescue missions around the world, from mountain rescue to sea evacuation. One of its most impressive aspects is its ability to airdrop rescue supplies, with remarkable precision, into areas inaccessible by other means. This feature has been crucial in many natural disasters, where time was of the essence in saving lives.

This aircraft model has also been equipped to serve as a flying ambulance, transporting casualties from combat zones or disaster sites. The C-130's ability to be rapidly reconfigured for different missions has made it an indispensable tool for armed forces and humanitarian organizations alike. It can be fitted with stretchers, advanced medical systems and even intensive care units, enabling medical care to be provided in-flight.

Beyond its transport and rescue role, the C-130 has been modified to perform other essential functions, such as firefighting, where it can drop tons of water or retardant to contain the flames. This versatility makes the C-130 a unique aircraft, capable of adapting to almost any emergency situation, be it humanitarian, military or rescue missions.

Rescue missions carried out by the C-130 have saved thousands of lives and demonstrated the value of this type of aircraft in critical situations. Its ability to intervene quickly, adapt to varied environments and provide vital support makes it a true pillar of air rescue operations. This aircraft symbolizes human ingenuity applied to improving rescue and recovery capabilities worldwide.

# Fact 66 - First commercial supersonic flight

On January 21, 1976, Concorde made its first supersonic commercial flight, marking a historic milestone in civil aviation. On that day, two Concordes took off simultaneously: one from London, bound for Bahrain, and the other from Paris, bound for Rio de Janeiro. These flights were not only Concorde's first commercial flights, but also the first to exceed the speed of sound with passengers on board, reaching a cruising speed of Mach 2, or around 2,180 km/h.

The Concorde, the fruit of collaboration between British and French engineers, was an unprecedented technological feat. With its slender design and delta wings, it was capable of crossing the Atlantic in just over three hours, a spectacular reduction in flight time compared with traditional subsonic aircraft. This ability to fly faster than sound while offering luxurious comfort made Concorde a symbol of elegance and innovation in the world of aviation.

However, Concorde's supersonic flight was not just about speed. It also required significant advances in materials and design. The extreme temperatures generated by Mach 2 flight called for the use of heat-resistant materials, such as a special aluminum alloy. In addition, the cabin design had to guarantee passenger comfort despite the challenges posed by these unique conditions.

The Concorde connected cities like New York and London in record time, becoming a popular choice for businessmen and celebrities looking to maximize their time. Despite high costs and operational challenges, for almost three decades the Concorde symbolized the pinnacle of air travel, before service was finally discontinued in 2003.

The Concorde legacy lives on, however, inspiring future generations of supersonic aircraft. Its first supersonic commercial flight not only redefined air travel expectations, but also demonstrated what was possible when engineering and innovation combined to push back the limits of human travel.

# Fact 67 - The plane that broke the speed record

The speed record for a manned aircraft is held by the SR-71 Blackbird, a strategic reconnaissance aircraft developed by Lockheed. On July 28, 1976, the SR-71 set a record that remains unmatched to this day: it reached the impressive speed of Mach 3.3, or around 3,540 km/h, at an altitude of 24,000 meters. This extraordinary speed enabled the Blackbird to cover immense distances in record time, while evading almost all types of missiles and fighter planes.

The SR-71 Blackbird, designed as part of Lockheed's Skunk Works program, was developed during the Cold War for reconnaissance missions over enemy territory. Its revolutionary design featured a structure made largely of titanium, a material needed to withstand the intense heat generated by high-speed flight. In addition, its unique aerodynamic shape and Pratt & Whitney J58 jet engines enabled the Blackbird to fly faster than any other aircraft of the time.

This speed record was not only a technological feat, but also a demonstration of US technological superiority during the Cold War. The SR-71 could gather crucial information in real time, and its ability to fly at altitudes and speeds inaccessible to other aircraft made it almost invulnerable to attack. Despite this, the Blackbird often had to fly over extremely dangerous areas, where enemy anti-aircraft defenses tried unsuccessfully to shoot it down.

The Blackbird flew for over three decades before being retired in 1998. However, its legacy continues to influence the design of modern aircraft, particularly those intended for reconnaissance and espionage missions. The SR-71 remains a powerful symbol of what aeronautical technology can achieve when pushed to its extreme limits.

The SR-71's speed record remains a benchmark in aviation history, illustrating the balance between technological innovation, military strategy and daring. It is a testament to human ingenuity and the will to surpass the boundaries of what is possible, even under extreme conditions.

# Fact 68 - First flight with a hydrogen engine

The first flight powered by a hydrogen engine marked a milestone in the history of aviation and the development of sustainable technologies. It was in 1988 that the Soviet Union carried out this revolutionary flight with a Tupolev Tu-155, a prototype based on the Tu-154, a popular commercial aircraft at the time. This experimental flight, carried out with an engine modified to run on liquid hydrogen, proved that hydrogen could be a viable alternative to traditional fossil fuels.

The use of hydrogen as an aviation fuel offers several significant advantages, not least a drastic reduction in greenhouse gas emissions, since hydrogen produces only water vapor during combustion. However, this flight also revealed the technical challenges involved in using this fuel, notably the storage and handling of liquid hydrogen, which requires extremely low temperatures to remain in its liquid state.

The Tupolev Tu-155 was designed with a special cryogenic tank to keep the hydrogen at around -253°C. The success of this flight demonstrated that it was possible to overcome the technical difficulties associated with the use of hydrogen in aviation. Nevertheless, this technology was not immediately adopted on a large scale, mainly due to the high cost and complexity of the infrastructure required for hydrogen storage and distribution.

This experimental flight in 1988 not only proved the feasibility of hydrogen as an aircraft fuel, but also laid the foundations for future research into sustainable aviation. Although other alternative fuels have since been explored, hydrogen continues to represent a promising option for a future where aviation could be significantly less polluting.

The Tupolev Tu-155 remains a milestone in aviation history, illustrating the first attempts to integrate more environmentally-friendly technologies. The flight inspired a wealth of research and innovation that continues to influence the development of the aircraft of the future.

# Fact 69 - The airplane that flies in the stratosphere

The Lockheed U-2 aircraft, often nicknamed the "Dragon Lady", is a technological feat capable of flying in the stratosphere, a region of the atmosphere between 10 and 50 kilometers above sea level. Designed during the Cold War, this aircraft was developed by the USA in the 1950s for reconnaissance missions at very high altitudes. Capable of reaching altitudes of over 21,000 meters, it made it possible to fly over enemy territory while remaining beyond the reach of traditional defense systems.

The development of the U-2 was a direct response to the need to gather precise information on Soviet military activities, particularly during periods of heightened tension. Its exceptionally high cruising altitude enabled it to overfly targets with great discretion, collecting crucial images and data thanks to advanced surveillance equipment for the time.

Flying the U-2 required specialized training, as its flight characteristics were extremely demanding. At such altitudes, there is little room for maneuver, making piloting a tricky business. The slightest error could result in loss of control. Pilots even wore pressure suits, similar to those used by astronauts, due to the low atmospheric pressure at these altitudes.

The Lockheed U-2 played a crucial role in a number of geopolitical crises, including the Cuban Missile Crisis in 1962. Images taken by this aircraft provided irrefutable evidence of Soviet missile installations in Cuba, helping to resolve the crisis. Its ability to fly in the stratosphere made it an incomparable strategic asset for the United States for many years.

Today, the U-2 remains in service, albeit modernized, and continues to carry out reconnaissance missions, proving the longevity and efficiency of its design. It remains a symbol of aeronautical innovation and of the human capacity to push back the limits of what is possible for defense and security.

# Fact 70 - The first fully-built wooden airplane

The De Havilland Mosquito, nicknamed "the Wooden Wonder", is one of the most emblematic aircraft of the Second World War. This British twin-engine aircraft is unique in that it was built entirely of wood, at a time when most military aircraft were made of metal. Its wooden design, mainly in birch plywood, not only reduced the weight of the aircraft, but also avoided the shortage of strategic materials such as aluminum.

The idea of building an airplane out of wood may have seemed anachronistic in the early 1940s, but it turned out to be a brilliant innovation. Geoffrey de Havilland, the chief designer, was able to exploit the lightness and strength of wood to create a fast, agile and versatile aircraft. The Mosquito could be configured for bombing and reconnaissance missions, or as a fighter-bomber, while outperforming many contemporary aircraft in terms of speed and maneuverability.

The Mosquito's wooden construction was not only a solution to wartime shortages, but also offered a tactical advantage. By flying at high speed at relatively low altitudes, the Mosquito could easily evade enemy radar, while being strong enough to withstand the stresses of combat missions. Artisan carpenters, rather than metalworkers, played a crucial role in the production of this aircraft, using manufacturing techniques more reminiscent of boat building than aircraft.

The Mosquito took part in many crucial missions during the war, including daring raids such as the one on the Amiens prison to free French Resistance fighters. Its ability to fly quickly and silently made it a weapon feared by the enemy, to the point of being dubbed "the most intrepid plane" by those who crossed its path.

The De Havilland Mosquito remains a fascinating example of wartime ingenuity and innovation, showing that sometimes the most effective solutions come from the most unexpected materials and methods. Far from being a mere relic of the past, this wooden aircraft left its mark on aviation history with its remarkable performance and daring design.

# Fact 71 - The plane that carried the most passengers

The Boeing 747, nicknamed the "Jumbo Jet", holds the record for the highest number of passengers carried on a single flight. This giant of the skies, introduced in the 1970s, revolutionized commercial aviation with its capacity, unrivalled at the time. The 747 was designed to meet the growing demand for large-scale air transport, enabling airlines to carry impressive numbers of passengers over long distances.

One of the most emblematic moments in Boeing 747 history took place during Operation Solomon in 1991, a humanitarian mission to evacuate thousands of Ethiopian Jews to Israel. A single 747 carried a record 1,088 passengers, well beyond its normal capacity. This exceptional flight demonstrated the 747's ability to be much more than just a commercial aircraft, becoming a symbol of hope and rescue for thousands of people.

The Boeing 747 marked a turning point in the aviation industry, not only for its size, but also for its technological innovations. It was the first commercial aircraft to feature an upper deck, initially conceived as a luxury space for first-class passengers. This feature became emblematic of the 747, contributing to its reputation as the "Queen of the Sky". In standard configuration, the 747 could carry over 500 passengers, making it ideal for high-density, long-haul flights.

Despite the arrival of new, more fuel-efficient models, the Boeing 747 remains a symbol of the golden age of commercial aviation. Its ability to carry large numbers of passengers made air travel accessible to more people around the world. The 747 not only redefined standards of capacity and comfort in aviation, it also played a crucial role in the democratization of air travel.

The Boeing 747, with its impressive capabilities, has been a key player in the evolution of commercial aviation. It proved that air travel could be both massive and efficient, while remaining safe and comfortable for passengers. This giant of the skies, which carried millions of passengers around the world, will forever be etched in aviation history for its extraordinary achievements.

# Fact 72 - First flight across a mountain range

The first flight across a mountain range was achieved by Swiss aviator Oskar Bider in 1913, a feat that marked a milestone in aviation history. Bider, who had already demonstrated his skills by flying over the Alps, decided to attempt a flight across the Pyrenees, a mountain range feared for its unpredictable weather conditions and high altitudes.

On July 13, 1913, Bider took off from Pau, France, in a single-engine Bleriot XI, a light but robust aircraft for its time. He crossed the Pyrenees to Madrid, Spain, covering a distance of some 500 kilometers. This daring flight, carried out at a time when navigation instruments were rudimentary, required exceptional mastery of the aircraft and a great ability to adapt to the complex air currents of the mountains.

This flight not only demonstrated the possibility of flying over large mountain ranges, but also paved the way for new air routes across the Alps and Pyrenees. Bider's success encouraged other aviators to attempt ever more ambitious flights, helping to expand the possibilities of both civil and military aviation.

Bider's feat also highlighted the importance of aviation in developing communications and transport between regions separated by major natural obstacles. By linking northern and southern Europe more efficiently, the flight symbolized a new era of connectivity, facilitating trade, travel and cultural exchange across the continent.

Oskar Bider became an aviation legend with this pioneering flight. He proved that limits once thought insurmountable could be overcome through determination, courage and innovation. His flight across the Pyrenees remains a milestone in aviation history, illustrating man's ability to overcome the challenges posed by nature through technology and ingenuity.

# Fact 73 - The plane with special landing gear

Aviation has always been a field where technical innovation plays a crucial role. One of the most singular advances in this field was the invention of the special landing gear, designed to enable aircraft to land in extreme conditions or on atypical terrain. Among the most remarkable examples, the Boeing YC-14 stands out. This experimental aircraft, developed in the 1970s, was equipped with landing gear enabling operations on very short or rudimentary runways, a major asset for military or humanitarian missions.

The YC-14's landing gear, consisting of wide, low-pressure tires, offered exceptional stability on unstable surfaces such as sand and mud. This system enabled the aircraft to considerably reduce its landing distance, a crucial capability in environments where traditional runways were non-existent or impassable. The ingenuity of this design lay in its combination of robustness and flexibility, adapted to the specific needs of certain missions.

In addition to its technical features, the YC-14's special landing gear marked a turning point in the design of Short Takeoff and Landing (STOL) aircraft. Thanks to this innovation, the YC-14 could take off and land on much shorter runways than those required for conventional aircraft in its class. This capability opened up new possibilities for flight operations in remote or undeveloped areas.

Although the YC-14 was never produced in series, the impact of its design has inspired many other aircraft projects, particularly in the cargo and military sectors. Today, the special landing gear concept is integrated into various aircraft models used for specific missions, particularly those requiring operations in difficult conditions.

The aircraft with special landing gear is a striking example of the importance of innovation in aviation. By pushing back the limits of what is possible in terms of landing and take-off, it has made it possible to overcome major logistical challenges and thus broadened the scope of modern aircraft. This Fact illustrates how a technical innovation can transform the capabilities of an aircraft and, by extension, the operational strategies of air missions.

# Fact 74 - First solo transpacific flight

The first solo trans-Pacific flight was one of the most daring and influential adventures in aviation history. The flight was made by American aviatrix Amelia Earhart, who achieved this feat in 1935, just eight years after becoming the first woman to fly solo across the Atlantic. This time, she set out to fly over the vast Pacific Ocean, an expanse made even more formidable by its unpredictable weather conditions and total isolation in the event of a breakdown.

Amelia Earhart took off from Honolulu, Hawaii, on January 11, 1935, at the controls of her Lockheed Vega 5B, a sturdy but rudimentary aircraft adapted for long solo flights. His goal was to reach Oakland, California, flying over the vastness of the Pacific Ocean without any outside help or refuelling. The flight was risky not only because of the vast distances involved, but also because of the changing weather conditions and the total absence of modern navigation systems.

After 18 hours of continuous flight, Earhart landed in Oakland on January 12, setting a new record for the longest and most daring solo flight to date. This flight of over 3,800 kilometers was a true feat of courage, determination and technical mastery. Earhart became an international heroine, proving that aviation could push back the limits of human endurance and aeronautical technology.

The success of this flight also marked a turning point in the history of solo aviation, inspiring other aviators to undertake transoceanic flights in the years that followed. Amelia Earhart's feat demonstrated that, despite extreme risks, determination and ingenuity could overcome the greatest challenges nature could impose. She left a lasting legacy, not only in aviation, but also in the history of human exploration.

This solo transpacific flight was much more than just a record: it symbolized man's (and woman's) ability to surpass themselves, to explore the unknown and achieve the impossible. Thanks to this feat, Amelia Earhart remains an emblematic figure in aviation, a pioneer who paved the way for new aerial explorations and the advancement of aviation technology.

# Fact 75 - The plane with the longest fuselage

The aircraft with the longest fuselage in the world is the Boeing 747-8, a modernized version of the famous 747, also nicknamed the "Jumbo Jet". Introduced in 2011, this aircraft is distinguished by its impressive fuselage, which reaches a length of 76.3 meters. This giant of the skies has been designed to meet the growing demand for passenger and freight transport worldwide, while incorporating modern technologies to improve efficiency and reduce operating costs.

The Boeing 747-8 is the fruit of decades of development and innovation in aeronautics. Its elongated structure accommodates up to 467 passengers in a typical three-class configuration, while offering exceptional cargo capacity. This version of the 747 has been equipped with more powerful and more fuel-efficient engines, the GEnx-2B67, which contribute to enhanced performance while reducing its ecological footprint.

One of the major challenges in designing the 747-8 was to maintain the aerodynamics and stability of an aircraft of this size. Engineers had to rethink certain aspects of the structure and materials to ensure that the elongated fuselage did not compromise the aircraft's safety or performance. The result is an aircraft which, despite its impressive length, retains remarkable manoeuvrability and meets the most stringent air safety standards.

This aircraft is mainly used by airlines for long-haul flights, linking international hubs in optimum comfort. It has also been adopted by cargo operators, who benefit from its ability to transport large quantities of goods over long distances. The Boeing 747-8 thus represents a milestone in the evolution of wide-body aircraft, combining tradition and innovation in a unique design.

With its imposing fuselage, the Boeing 747-8 has become a symbol of power and technological progress in commercial aviation. It embodies the aviation industry's ability to push back the boundaries of what is possible, creating ever larger, more efficient aircraft that are better adapted to global needs.

# Fact 76 - First plane to use biofuels

In 2008, a landmark event changed the history of modern aviation when Virgin Atlantic's Boeing 747 became the first commercial aircraft to use biofuels for a flight. This flight, from London to Amsterdam, proved that aviation could move towards more environmentally-friendly solutions, by partially replacing traditional kerosene with fuels from renewable sources, such as vegetable oils.

The Boeing 747's number one engine was fuelled by a blend containing 20% biofuels derived from babassu nuts and coconuts, while the other three engines used conventional kerosene. The aim of the experiment was to test the feasibility of using biofuels in aviation, while minimizing the risks associated with in-flight performance. The results were encouraging, paving the way for further research into the integration of these sustainable fuels into commercial flights.

The biofuels used on this flight were chosen for their compatibility with existing engines, without the need for major modifications. They also had the advantage of reducing $CO_2$ emissions compared with fossil fuels, a crucial aspect for the aeronautical industry seeking solutions to reduce its carbon footprint. The success of this flight demonstrated that it is possible to reduce environmental impact without compromising flight safety or efficiency.

Following this pioneering experience, many airlines and aircraft manufacturers have stepped up their efforts to develop and certify biofuels on a large scale. The aim is to make commercial flights increasingly environmentally friendly, while meeting the stringent requirements of aviation in terms of safety, performance and profitability.

This first flight using biofuels represents a turning point in aviation history, demonstrating that the industry can move towards more sustainable practices without sacrificing performance. It also illustrates the importance of innovation in the aviation sector to meet the environmental challenges of the 21st century.

# Fact 77 - The plane that can land on a river

On January 15, 2009, the world witnessed an extraordinary aeronautical feat when US Airways Flight 1549, piloted by Captain Chesley "Sully" Sullenberger, made an emergency water landing on the Hudson River in New York. This Airbus A320, after losing power on both engines following a collision with birds shortly after take-off, managed to land safely on the water, saving the lives of all 155 people on board.

The plane was not specifically designed to land on a river, but the pilot's quick decision and expertise made the landing possible. The choice of the Hudson River as an improvised landing strip was motivated by the absence of landing fields nearby and the need to minimize risks to passengers and city residents. The water acted as a shock absorber, allowing the aircraft to slow down safely.

This incident highlighted the Airbus A320's ability to withstand extreme conditions, even in unforeseen emergency situations. The crew applied emergency procedures with remarkable precision, deploying emergency slides for water evacuation and ensuring that all passengers were safe. This event has been dubbed "the miracle of the Hudson", due to the absence of casualties despite the gravity of the situation.

The ditching on the Hudson River not only demonstrated the importance of rigorous pilot training, but also the robustness of modern aircraft in unexpected situations. Since that incident, improvements have been made to emergency management protocols and aircraft design to enhance their ability to cope with similar situations.

This feat will go down in aviation history as one of the most impressive demonstrations of a crew's skill and composure in the face of a critical situation. It also serves as a reminder that, even without specialized equipment, an aircraft can, in expert hands, perform unexpected feats.

# Fact 78 - The quietest flight ever recorded

In 2019, a historic test flight took place with NASA's X-57 Maxwell experimental aircraft, designed to be one of the quietest aircraft ever built. This electric aircraft, using motors powered by lithium-ion batteries, marked a turning point in aviation history by demonstrating that flight could be achieved almost silently, a major breakthrough for the future of sustainable aviation.

The X-57 Maxwell is a light aircraft with 14 electric motors distributed along its wings. Unlike traditional aircraft with combustion engines, electric power almost completely eliminates engine noise, making flight much quieter. The absence of vibration and combustion noise also contributes to a smoother, more comfortable flying experience.

In its first tests, the X-57 showed a dramatic reduction in noise, particularly during critical phases of flight such as take-off and landing, when traditional aircraft are generally the noisiest. This innovation is particularly important for urban areas where noise pollution is a growing concern, and where quiet aircraft could revolutionize the way airports are integrated into cities.

The aim of the X-57 Maxwell was not only to prove that an electric aircraft could fly, but also to show that aviation could be transformed into a more environmentally-friendly industry, without sacrificing performance. The success of these experimental flights has paved the way for future developments in the field of electric commercial aircraft, where silence is also an asset in terms of passenger comfort.

To this day, the X-57 Maxwell remains one of the most promising examples of what the future of aviation could look like: quiet, clean, environmentally-friendly flights, marking a milestone in the evolution of aeronautical technologies.

# Fact 79 - First flight over the South Atlantic

The first flight over the South Atlantic, a milestone in aviation history, was achieved by Portuguese aviators Gago Coutinho and Sacadura Cabral in 1922. This epic crossing between Lisbon, Portugal, and Rio de Janeiro, Brazil, made history not only as the first flight to link the continents of Europe and South America, but also as a remarkable technical feat for its time.

Coutinho and Cabral used a Fairey III seaplane, specially modified for this mission. They had to cope with extremely difficult weather conditions, frequent storms and the technical challenges of navigating such a long distance without modern technology. The flight lasted several weeks, requiring several stopovers and the replacement of their aircraft after a forced landing in the open sea.

The key element of this crossing was the use of a sextant specially adapted for aerial navigation, developed by Gago Coutinho himself. This instrument enabled more precise navigation, which was crucial for maintaining course over such a long distance across an ocean with no visual landmarks. This innovation paved the way for future transoceanic flights, proving that safe, reliable air travel could be achieved even over great distances.

Coutinho and Cabral's South Atlantic crossing was an internationally celebrated feat, highlighting the technological advances and courage required to overcome the challenges posed by such an audacious flight. The event is often compared to Charles Lindbergh's North Atlantic crossing, made five years later, although Coutinho and Cabral's flight received far less media coverage.

This feat remains an important milestone in aviation history, symbolizing the ingenuity and determination of the pioneers who pushed back the boundaries of what was considered possible. Their success set a new standard for long-distance flight, inspiring subsequent generations of aviators to continue exploring the skies beyond known horizons.

# Fact 80 - The plane that reached the highest altitude

The aircraft that holds the record for the highest altitude reached is the Lockheed U-2, an American reconnaissance aircraft designed during the Cold War. This legendary model, nicknamed the "Dragon Lady", was developed for high-altitude surveillance missions, capable of flying at over 21,000 meters, or almost 70,000 feet. This extraordinary altitude enabled it to evade enemy radar and defense systems, making its missions particularly effective.

The U-2 was designed to fly over hostile territory while gathering crucial information thanks to its advanced reconnaissance equipment. Its ability to fly this high played a vital role during the Cuban Missile Crisis in 1962, when it provided crucial photographic evidence of Soviet missile installations on the island. This mission illustrates the strategic importance of the maximum altitude an aircraft can reach.

One of the most impressive aspects of the U-2 is its lightweight structure and extremely long wings, designed to maintain lift at altitudes where the air is very thin. However, this design made the U-2 very difficult to fly, especially during the take-off and landing phases, where a small mistake could be fatal. The pilots, specially trained for these missions, wore pressurized suits similar to those used in space.

The Lockheed U-2 remains in service today, although it has been modernized over the decades to adapt to new technologies. Its endurance, ability to reach extreme altitudes and crucial role in sensitive intelligence missions have made it an iconic aircraft in military aviation. Not only has it pushed back the limits of flight altitude, it has also left its mark on history, influencing the course of several major geopolitical events.

The feat of the U-2 underlines aviation's relentless quest to push back the frontiers of the possible. By reaching the highest skies, this aircraft ushered in a new era of aerial surveillance and reconnaissance, proving that even the most extreme altitudes can be conquered with technology and human ingenuity.

# Fact 81 - First photographic reconnaissance flight

The first photographic reconnaissance flight dates back to the First World War, a period when military aviation was still in its infancy. The idea of capturing images of the battlefield from the air was seen as a major strategic advance. By 1914, British army pilots were using aircraft such as the Royal Aircraft Factory B.E.2 to photograph enemy positions, marking the beginning of a new era in modern warfare.

These early photographic missions were rudimentary. Pilots and observers carried heavy, unwieldy cameras in the open cockpit of their aircraft. Images were taken at relatively low altitudes, exposing the aircraft to enemy fire. Despite these dangers, the photographs obtained proved invaluable for military planning, enabling commanders to see, for the first time, the deployment of troops and enemy fortifications with unprecedented precision.

One of the first significant photographic reconnaissance missions took place during the Battle of the Marne in 1914. Aerial images revealed that German troops were attempting to outflank Allied forces, enabling Allied commanders to readjust their forces in time to counter this maneuver. This event proved the importance of aerial photography, which rapidly became a crucial element of military strategy.

As the war progressed, photographic reconnaissance techniques and equipment improved. Aircraft were equipped with more powerful cameras, capable of taking images at higher altitudes, thus reducing the risks for pilots. What's more, images were developed rapidly in the field, enabling analysts to map enemy positions in near-real time, revolutionizing the way battles were fought.

The development of photographic reconnaissance marked a turning point in the history of aviation and warfare. What began as a simple innovation quickly became standard practice in all modern armies, evolving with technological advances to become an essential tool of military intelligence. The first photographic reconnaissance flight not only changed warfare, but also ushered in a new era in aerial observation, which remains crucial in contemporary conflicts.

# Fact 82 - The airplane with a rotary engine

One of the most innovative developments in aviation in the early 20th century was the introduction of rotary engines, a technology that marked a turning point in aircraft performance. A rotary engine is unique in that not only does the crankshaft remain fixed, but the entire engine block rotates around it. This design offered natural, efficient engine cooling, a crucial advantage in open-cockpit aircraft where air cooling was essential.

The famous French fighter, the Nieuport 11, used during the First World War, is an emblematic example of an aircraft fitted with a rotary engine. This type of engine, often from the Gnome and Le Rhône families, gave the plane exceptional maneuverability, a considerable asset in close air combat. Pilots particularly appreciated the aircraft's responsiveness, although the gyroscopic torque generated by the engine's rotation made maneuvering more complex, especially during tight turns.

Rotary engines were popular among light fighters, not least because they offered an excellent power-to-weight ratio. The 130 hp Clerget 9B rotary engine was used on the Sopwith Camel, one of the most feared British fighters of the First World War. Thanks to its rotary design, this engine enabled the Sopwith Camel to climb rapidly and make quick turns, giving pilots a significant tactical advantage in aerial combat.

However, this technology also had its limitations. Rotary engines tended to consume large quantities of oil, which they often ejected in the form of mist, inconveniencing pilots. What's more, their complex design made maintenance difficult, and their lifespan was generally shorter than that of in-line engines, which would eventually supplant them after the war.

The era of rotary engines was brief but influential. Although they were soon replaced by more efficient and easier-to-maintain engines, they played a crucial role in the evolution of military aviation and helped define modern aerial tactics. Their legacy lies in the way they enabled the aircraft of that era to push back the limits of flight, having a lasting influence on fighter aircraft design and aviation history.

# Fact 83 - First theft inside a building

The idea of flying an airplane inside a building may seem incongruous, but that's precisely what happened at the 1900 Paris World's Fair. Clément Ader, an engineer and pioneer of French aviation, was the man behind this feat. Known for his groundbreaking work in aeronautics, Ader pulled off a unique feat by taking off his aircraft, the Ader Avion III, inside the Palais de l'Industrie, a vast glass and iron structure built especially for the occasion.

This domestic flight was first and foremost a demonstration of technical progress in aviation. The Ader Avion III, powered by two steam engines, was as impressive as it was complex for its time. Although the flight itself was short and limited by the constraints of the enclosed space, it made a lasting impression by showing that it was possible to get a heavier-than-air aircraft off the ground in such a restricted environment.

The interior environment of the Palais de l'Industrie presented a number of challenges. Controlling the plane in a confined space required extreme precision, and air currents were particularly difficult to manage. Nevertheless, Ader succeeded in keeping his plane aloft for a short distance, once again demonstrating his ingenuity. This flight not only enhanced his reputation as a pioneer, but also contributed to the advancement of aviation by proving the feasibility of low-level flight in confined spaces.

Clément Ader's achievement paved the way for new experiments in aviation, notably those concerning aircraft control and stability in a variety of environments. Although this indoor flight was not as spectacular as the great crossings or high-altitude flights, it remains a milestone in aviation history. It also inspired other inventors and engineers to explore new possibilities for the future of aviation.

Clément Ader's interior flight remains a testament to the genius and vision of the early aviation pioneers. He proved that even the most unusual spaces could be used to explore the limits of aeronautical technology, and left a lasting imprint on aviation history.

# Fact 84 - The plane with the most flexible wings

Aviation has always been a field where human ingenuity is put to the test, and one of the most fascinating examples of this creativity is the development of aircraft with extremely flexible wings. One of the pioneers in this field is the Boeing 787 Dreamliner, which has pushed back the boundaries of aeronautical engineering by incorporating wings designed to be particularly flexible.

The wings of the Boeing 787 are made mainly of composite materials, which give them far greater flexibility than traditional aluminum wings. This flexibility is not only a technical feat, but also plays a crucial role in improving the aircraft's performance. Indeed, flexible wings can absorb some of the turbulence, reducing the vibrations felt by passengers and increasing aerodynamic efficiency.

The flexibility of the Dreamliner's wings also helps reduce fuel consumption. As the wings bend slightly under air pressure in flight, they dynamically adapt to atmospheric conditions, minimizing drag and optimizing aerodynamics. This feature makes the Boeing 787 not only more comfortable for passengers, but also more environmentally-friendly and economical to operate.

The design of these flexible wings required years of research and development. Engineers had to overcome many challenges, not least the structural strength and durability of the composite materials used. However, the results lived up to expectations, making the Boeing 787 a symbol of innovation in modern aviation.

This development marks a milestone in the evolution of commercial aircraft. By incorporating advanced technologies such as flexible wings, the aviation industry continues to push back the frontiers of what is possible, creating aircraft that are not only more efficient, but also more environmentally friendly. The story of the Dreamliner shows how innovation and experimentation can transform seemingly simple concepts, such as flexible wings, into major assets for the future of aviation.

# Fact 85 - First flight with blind passengers

On April 29, 1932, a milestone in aviation history took place: the first flight made up entirely of blind passengers. This pioneering initiative was organized by the Royal National Institute of Blind People (RNIB) in the UK, with the aim of demonstrating that commercial aviation was accessible to all, regardless of physical ability.

This historic flight took place aboard a De Havilland DH.89 Dragon Rapide, a twin-engine aircraft capable of carrying eight passengers. The aircraft took off from London's Croydon airfield for a scenic flight over the English countryside. On board were eight blind passengers, all members of the RNIB, who had been specially invited for this unique experience. The flight was a complete success, proving that blind people can travel by plane as safely and comfortably as any other passenger.

The pilot, well aware of the importance of this flight, had prepared a detailed commentary which he broadcast during the flight, describing the landscapes overflown. Passengers, although unable to see, were able to participate in the experience thanks to these descriptions, reinforcing the idea that air travel could be an inclusive and accessible activity.

This event not only raised public awareness of the capabilities of blind people, but also inspired improvements in aircraft design to better accommodate passengers with special needs. Efforts to make aviation more accessible accelerated after this flight, laying the foundations for many innovations that continue to benefit travelers with reduced mobility or other disabilities.

The 1932 flight marked a turning point in commercial aviation, illustrating that the skies were open to all, without distinction. It goes down in history not only as a technical feat, but also as a symbol of social progress, showing that inclusion and accessibility are fundamental values in the evolution of air transport.

# Fact 86 - The plane that flew over every continent

The remarkable feat of flying over every continent on Earth was accomplished by the Boeing 747, one of the most emblematic aircraft in aviation history. This aircraft, nicknamed the "Jumbo Jet", played a crucial role in the democratization of long-distance air travel, capable of carrying large numbers of passengers over very long distances.

The Boeing 747, in its various versions, has been used by numerous airlines to connect destinations in every corner of the globe. Thanks to its impressive range, this aircraft was the first to make commercial flights between distant continents without requiring numerous refueling stops. Among the many records set by the 747, that of flying over every continent, including Antarctica, illustrates its ability to operate in varied and sometimes extreme conditions.

The 747 flew over Antarctica on special air tourism missions, allowing its passengers to contemplate the vast icy expanses of this rarely visited continent. These flights, organized mainly from Australia, demonstrated the aircraft's reliability in extreme climatic conditions, where very low temperatures and powerful winds pose unique challenges.

In North America and Europe, the 747 connected major cities across the Atlantic, becoming an essential air bridge between the two continents. In Asia and Africa, it has opened up routes to remote destinations, stimulating trade and tourism. In South America, its capabilities have made it possible to fly over the Andes, while in Australia, it has linked the country's major cities to the rest of the world.

This aircraft, a symbol of the power of the modern aeronautics industry, remains etched in history for having connected all continents regularly and reliably. The Boeing 747 not only flew across the globe, it also brought people and cultures closer together, making our world more accessible than ever before.

# Fact 87 - First flight through a snowstorm

The first documented flight through a snowstorm was a milestone in aviation history, demonstrating the ability of aircraft to cope with extreme weather conditions. This feat dates back to the early days of aviation, when pilots often ventured into the unknown without the aid of modern navigation systems.

One of the most famous flights took place in 1925, when a young American pilot, Carl Ben Eielson, set out to fly through a snowstorm in Alaska. Tasked with transporting mail in treacherous conditions, Eielson took to the skies in a small open-cockpit plane, braving freezing temperatures and near-zero visibility. The flight proved not only his courage, but also the resilience of aircraft at the time, which were still largely made of wood and canvas.

In those days, weather forecasting was rudimentary, and pilots often had to rely on instinct and experience to navigate safely. Snowstorms posed a particular challenge, reducing visibility to a few meters and icing up wings and engines, making flight extremely hazardous. Nevertheless, Eielson succeeded in his mission, becoming a local hero and an icon of Arctic aviation.

This daring flight highlighted the dangers faced by aviation pioneers, but also showed the potential of aviation to link isolated regions, even in severe climatic conditions. The heroism of pilots like Eielson paved the way for technological advances, notably in aircraft de-icing and improved navigation systems, which made flying in winter conditions safer.

Today, aircraft are designed to cope with a wide variety of weather conditions, including the most violent snowstorms. But the feat of Eielson and his contemporaries remains a poignant reminder of the risks early pilots took to explore the skies, often in spite of the dangers inherent in nature itself.

# Fact 88 - The airplane that turns into a glider

One of the most fascinating concepts in aviation is that of aircraft capable of transforming into gliders, a feat based on technical ingenuity and a thorough understanding of aerodynamics. These aircraft are designed to fly autonomously with engines, but if necessary, they can transform into gliders, using only air currents to maintain their flight.

One of the first outstanding examples of this technology was the Me 163 Komet, a German fighter used during the Second World War. This small rocket plane, capable of impressive speeds, quickly ran out of fuel. Once its tanks were empty, it transformed into a glider, enabling the pilot to continue his flight and land safely. This ability to glide after powered flight represented a strategic breakthrough, offering unprecedented flexibility for combat missions.

This concept has found applications beyond the military sphere. In aerospace research, some experimental aircraft are designed to use this dual capability. For example, the X-24B, a NASA experimental aircraft of the 1970s, could fly at high speed with its rocket engines, then glide to land, simulating the descent characteristics of future space shuttles.

The advantages of this transformation lie in the aircraft's ability to carry out missions using a minimum of fuel, particularly during the final phases of flight when the engines can be shut down for a silent, precise landing. This not only saves fuel, but also minimizes noise and reduces the ecological footprint of the flight.

Today, the idea of a plane that can transform itself into a glider continues to inspire engineers and designers, who see this technology as a way of making aviation more efficient and environmentally friendly. This fascinating concept remains an emblematic example of human ingenuity and our perpetual quest to push back the limits of flight.

# Fact 89 - First flight with an all-female crew

The first flight with an all-female crew marks a significant turning point in aviation history, symbolizing not only a technical breakthrough but also an important step towards gender equality in a field long dominated by men. This historic event took place on January 29, 1934, when pilot Edna Gardner Whyte, accompanied by two other women, completed a flight from Oakland, California, to Miami, Florida.

This flight, aboard a Ford Trimotor biplane, demonstrated the competence and professionalism of women in a field where their presence was still rare. At the time, the role of women in aviation was often limited to that of stewardesses or secretaries, and to see an all-female crew was a real revolution. The success of this flight paved the way for greater recognition of women pilots, and inspired many others to pursue careers in aviation.

The members of this crew were not only pioneers, but also role models for future generations. Their competence put an end to many prejudices, proving that women could handle all the tasks involved in a flight, from navigation to emergency management, with as much rigor and success as their male counterparts.

In the decades that followed, the number of women in aviation continued to grow, with famous examples such as Amelia Earhart and Jacqueline Cochran, who in turn broke new barriers. Not only did these women contribute to technical progress in aviation, they also played a crucial role in social transformation, redefining what it meant to be a pilot.

Today, flights with all-female crews are no longer an exception but a common reality, a testament to changing attitudes and the growing acceptance of diversity in aviation. Yet this historic achievement in 1934 remains a memorable milestone, celebrated for having paved the way for all the women who have since taken their place in cockpits the world over.

# Fact 90 - The airplane with the longest range

The aircraft that holds the record for longest range is the Boeing 777-200LR, capable of covering incredible distances non-stop. This model was designed to push back the limits of long-distance flight. In 2005, it made a historic flight from Hong Kong to London, via the Pacific Ocean, North America and the Atlantic, covering over 21,600 kilometers in almost 23 hours.

The secret of this exceptional range lies in the combination of its aerodynamic design, high-performance engines and high-capacity fuel tank. The Boeing 777-200LR can carry up to 301 passengers while maintaining outstanding fuel efficiency, making it ideal for ultra-long-haul flights. It has been designed with larger wings and lighter materials, optimizing range and fuel consumption.

The aircraft is also equipped with General Electric GE90-115B engines, the most powerful commercial aircraft engines ever built. These engines enable the 777-200LR not only to fly further, but also to take off with maximum load, increasing operational flexibility for airlines using it on very long routes, sometimes far from major airport hubs.

The Boeing 777-200LR was developed in response to the airline industry's growing demand for direct flights between distant cities, eliminating the need for multiple stopovers and reducing overall travel time. This aircraft has opened up new direct connections between destinations on the other side of the globe, making the world even more accessible.

By crossing record distances, the 777-200LR not only demonstrated Boeing's technological capabilities, it also redefined what it means to travel very long distances. Today, although other airplanes have emerged, the Boeing 777-200LR remains a benchmark for autonomy, and continues to connect cities around the world more efficiently and rapidly.

# Fact 91 - First flight of a single-wing aircraft

One of the most daring concepts in aviation history is the single-wing aircraft, also known as the "flying wing". The first successful flight of a single-wing aircraft dates back to the 1940s, with the development of the Northrop N-1M, an American prototype designed by visionary engineer Jack Northrop. This aircraft marked a turning point in aircraft design, abandoning the traditional fuselage-and-tailplane structure for a form in which the single wing acted as the main body.

The Northrop N-1M, nicknamed the "Flying Wing", made its first flight in 1940. This innovative machine demonstrated that the aerodynamics of the flying wing offered several advantages, including a significant reduction in drag and improved lift, which could potentially improve aircraft fuel efficiency. However, control of the aircraft presented challenges, not least due to the absence of a conventional rudder, making in-flight stability more difficult to maintain.

Northrop's flying wing was equipped with two propeller engines and a unique aerodynamic configuration that redistributed forces to maintain balance in flight. Although the N-1M's performance was encouraging, it was still a prototype, and improvements were needed to make the concept fully operational. This project laid the foundations for the future development of this type of aircraft, leading to more advanced models such as the Northrop YB-35 and the famous B-2 Spirit, the US Air Force's stealth bomber.

The idea of a single-wing aircraft was revolutionary for its time, and although the concept did not immediately find commercial application, it had a lasting influence on the design of modern military aircraft. By reducing external surfaces and integrating flight controls into the wing, these aircraft showed that it was possible to build more discreet, fuel-efficient aircraft.

Today, the principles discovered through these first flying wing flights are being applied in various fields of aviation, including the design of stealth aircraft and drones. The Northrop N-1M remains a striking example of how innovation and the desire to push back the limits of technology can open up new avenues in aeronautics.

# Fact 92 - Aircraft designed to carry submarines

In the 1930s, as the world's great powers competed in military ingenuity, the idea of an aircraft capable of transporting submarines emerged in the minds of Soviet engineers. The ambitious project, supported by the Soviet Union, aimed to combine air capabilities with naval power by developing an aircraft capable of moving small submarines from one point to another, thus expanding the army's tactical possibilities.

The Tupolev TB-3 aircraft, a heavy bomber already in service at the time, was chosen as the basic platform for this project. Modified to meet the specific needs of submarine transport, the TB-3 was to carry a midget submarine, the Shchuka, under its fuselage. This concept was intended to enable Soviet forces to deploy submarines in remote and difficult-to-access areas, without having to sail them over long distances.

Soviet engineers adapted the TB-3 by reinforcing its structure to support the additional weight of the submarine, which was attached to the underside of the aircraft by a specially designed winch and cable system. The submarine was small in size, with limited autonomy, but sufficiently effective for reconnaissance and rapid attack missions once deployed. This innovation offered the Soviet Union a unique means of projecting its military power beyond the usual geographical limits.

Despite initial hopes, the project was never fully operational. The technical and logistical challenges, in particular the difficulty of maintaining the aircraft's stability in flight with such a heavy and cumbersome load, proved too great to overcome with the technologies available at the time. The TB-3, though robust, could never fully fulfill the role for which it had been modified, and the project was eventually abandoned.

Nevertheless, the project remains a fascinating example of the creativity and ingenuity deployed by military engineers. It illustrates the constant efforts to push back the limits of what is possible in the field of aviation and military strategy, even if not every idea becomes reality. Today, the TB-3 and the Shchuka submarine remain symbols of this quest for radical innovation in a world in the throes of technological change.

# Fact 93 - First flight with passengers in reduced space

The first flight with passengers in confined spaces dates back to the 1920s, when commercial aviation was still in its infancy. Aircraft of that era were not designed for the comfort we enjoy today. In Fact, the first passengers traveled in extremely rudimentary conditions, often in narrow cabins, without the luxury of modern amenities such as comfortable seats or even toilets.

One of the most emblematic examples of this type of flight is the Junkers F.13, a German aircraft introduced in 1919. Designed mainly in metal, the F.13 was a low-wing, single-engine aircraft capable of carrying up to four passengers. However, space on board was very limited. Seating was rudimentary, and passengers often had to cram into a narrow compartment, with no separation between them and the pilot. This flight marked a milestone in the evolution of commercial air transport, despite the obvious lack of comfort.

Passengers, often adventurers or intrepid businessmen, accepted these Spartan travel conditions for the speed offered by the airplane compared to other means of transport of the time. Despite its limitations, the Junkers F.13 was a commercial success, paving the way for regular flights between major European cities. It demonstrated that aviation could not only be a reality for passenger transport, but also become a viable alternative to long journeys by train or ship.

This type of reduced-space flight also laid the foundations for the design of passenger cabins for decades to come. Engineers took note of criticism of the lack of comfort and began working on solutions to improve the passenger experience. In this way, every flight in these restricted conditions has helped shape modern commercial aviation, where passenger comfort has become a priority.

Today, it's fascinating to think that the first air passengers traveled in such rudimentary conditions, while comfort and space are now essential elements of air travel. This historical Fact is a reminder of the modest beginnings of commercial aviation and the distance covered since then.

# Fact 94 - The plane with the smallest carbon footprint

The aircraft with the smallest carbon footprint to date is the Solar Impulse 2, a revolutionary aircraft designed to demonstrate the potential of renewable energies in aviation. Designed by the team led by Swiss pioneers Bertrand Piccard and André Borschberg, this solar-powered aircraft has become a powerful symbol of the possibility of carbon-free aviation. Powered exclusively by solar energy, Solar Impulse 2 consumes no fossil fuels and therefore produces no CO2 emissions.

The Solar Impulse 2 is covered with 17,248 solar cells that power its electric motors, enabling the plane to fly day and night without interruption. In 2016, this aircraft achieved a historic feat by flying around the world in several stages, covering more than 40,000 kilometers without using a single drop of fuel. This trip marked a turning point in aviation history, proving that renewable energies could be used effectively for long-distance flights.

The ingenuity behind the Solar Impulse 2 lies in its ultralight design and exceptional energy efficiency. The aircraft, made from ultra-light composite materials, weighs around 2,300 kg, roughly the same as a medium-sized car. This lightness, combined with optimized aerodynamics and a large wingspan, ensures minimal energy consumption, which is crucial for maintaining continuous flight from captured solar energy.

The impact of Solar Impulse 2 goes far beyond the boundaries of aviation. Its success has encouraged the research and development of sustainable technologies in various fields, showing that an ecological approach is not only a necessity, but also an opportunity for innovation. This aircraft represents the future of more environmentally-friendly aviation, paving the way for technologies that could ultimately reduce the carbon footprint of the entire aviation industry.

The story of Solar Impulse 2 is a powerful reminder of the human capacity to overcome technical challenges to build a cleaner future. Far from being a mere prototype, this aircraft embodies a sustainable vision of flight, where clean, inexhaustible solar energy could well be the key to drastically reducing the environmental impact of global aviation.

# Fact 95 - First flight with a nuclear reactor

The first flight of a nuclear-powered aircraft dates back to the 1950s, a period of intense exploration of nuclear technologies. The American Nuclear Powered Aircraft (NPA) program led to the design of the Convair NB-36H experimental aircraft, a bomber modified to carry a nuclear reactor on board. The aim of this project was to explore the feasibility of flights of virtually unlimited duration powered by nuclear energy.

The Convair NB-36H, nicknamed the "Crusader", was not a purely nuclear aircraft in terms of propulsion. Indeed, the on-board reactor did not directly supply power to the engines, but its main role was to test the radiation shield and measure the effects of the reactor in flight. Between 1955 and 1957, the aircraft made 47 test flights, demonstrating the technical feasibility of safely transporting a nuclear reactor, although the concept was never applied to commercial or military aircraft due to the associated risks.

The on-board reactor weighed several tons, and the aircraft was modified to support this extra load while maintaining thick shielding to protect the crew from radiation. The cockpit of the NB-36H, for example, was surrounded by a 12-ton lead shield to absorb the radiation emitted by the operating nuclear reactor.

Despite these technical achievements, the nuclear aircraft program was eventually abandoned. The challenges posed by nuclear waste management, the risks of contamination in the event of a crash, and rapid advances in conventional jet propulsion technologies tipped the balance in favor of less risky solutions. Nevertheless, the Convair NB-36H remains a fascinating testament to the technological daring of the time, illustrating the boundless ambitions of aviation during the Cold War.

Nevertheless, the project left a lasting imprint on the history of aviation and nuclear power, showing just how far engineers were prepared to go to push back the limits of what was possible. The NB-36H embodies this period when the imagination of engineers and the possibilities offered by nuclear technology seemed to open up new frontiers, even if these ultimately proved too dangerous to cross.

# Fact 96 - The plane that flew with broken wings

The story of the plane that flew with partially broken wings is an extraordinary example of mechanical resilience and pilot skill. The incident occurred during a test flight of the famous Lockheed U-2, a high-altitude reconnaissance aircraft designed during the Cold War. Thanks to its unique design, the U-2 could fly at altitudes inaccessible to fighter jets of the time, but it was also known for its delicacy in flight, particularly with regard to its thin, long wings.

During a test mission, one of the U-2 prototypes suffered an in-flight shock that damaged part of its wings. Such a situation would normally have led to disaster, as the wings play a crucial role not only in maintaining altitude, but also in the aircraft's stability. However, against all the odds, the pilot managed to keep the plane airborne, skilfully using the controls to compensate for the loss of aerodynamic efficiency caused by the damage.

The U-2's ability to keep flying despite partially broken wings is due to its robust design and the structural flexibility of its wings. Although long and fragile in appearance, the wings were designed to withstand considerable stress, enabling the aircraft to remain airborne even in such critical conditions. The pilot, for his part, had to demonstrate exceptional skill to manage the imbalances and bring the plane back to a safe altitude.

This miraculous flight not only demonstrated the quality of the U-2's design, but also reinforced the reputation of Lockheed's engineers and test pilots, known for their work on highly confidential projects. Although the aircraft subsequently underwent major repairs, the incident led to further improvements in the U-2's design, strengthening some of its critical parts to prevent similar accidents in the future.

The plane that flew with broken wings is a testament to human ingenuity and the ability to overcome seemingly insurmountable challenges, even in the sky. This event marked an astonishing chapter in aviation history, where the combination of advanced technology and human skill averted a certain crash, making this aircraft a symbol of resilience and engineering.

# Fact 97 - First experimental flight for medicine

The first experimental flight dedicated to medicine marked a turning point in the use of aviation for crucial scientific advances. This historic flight, carried out at the beginning of the 20th century, was designed to study the effects of altitude on the human body, particularly with regard to breathing and blood circulation. At the time, knowledge of the physiological effects of flight was still limited, and this type of research was essential to ensure the safety of pilots and future passengers.

On board the plane, doctors and scientists carried instruments to measure the blood pressure, breathing and other vital signs of the volunteers taking part in the experiment. The plane gradually climbed in altitude, reaching levels never before achieved by medical experiments. The results of these measurements provided valuable data that contributed to understanding the risks associated with altitude, in particular hypoxia, a condition caused by the lack of oxygen at high altitude.

One of the most important discoveries of this flight was the identification of the symptoms of altitude sickness in the pilots. These symptoms, such as dizziness, nausea and mental confusion, were poorly understood prior to this experiment. Thanks to the data collected, the researchers were able to develop recommendations for improving the safety of high-altitude flights, including the use of oxygen masks and cabin pressurization, which have become standard in modern aviation.

This experimental flight also improved emergency medical practices in extreme environments, paving the way for air evacuation of patients and rapid transport of medicines and medical supplies. It demonstrated that aviation can play a vital role in medicine, not only in wartime, but also in civilian life.

Ultimately, this first experimental flight for medicine laid the foundations for a new discipline: aviation medicine. This discipline has evolved to become a mainstay of aviation safety and medical care, perfectly illustrating how aviation has helped to push back the frontiers of science and improve human life.

# Fact 98 - The plane with infinite autonomy

The idea of an aircraft capable of flying without ever needing to refuel once seemed purely utopian. Yet such a feat has been achieved thanks to technological advances in solar energy. The Solar Impulse 2 solar airplane completed a historic flight in 2016, covering 42,000 kilometers around the globe without using a single drop of fossil fuel. This feat was made possible by wings covered with ultra-efficient solar panels, capable of supplying the energy needed to propel the aircraft.

The Solar Impulse 2 is equipped with light but powerful batteries, which store the solar energy captured during the day, enabling the plane to continue flying even during the night. This ingenious system has given the plane theoretically infinite autonomy, as long as the sun shines to recharge its batteries. The concept of infinite autonomy therefore lies not in inexhaustible capacity, but in total dependence on a renewable energy source.

Flying such an aircraft nevertheless poses unique challenges. Long-distance flying requires not only reliable technology, but also exceptional mental and physical preparation for the crew. During this round-the-world flight, the pilots had to manage extended periods of wakefulness and solitude, while remaining focused on manually piloting the aircraft, often in difficult weather conditions.

The impact of this flight goes far beyond aviation. It demonstrates the viability of renewable energies, and encourages us to rethink the way we envisage the future of air transport. The Solar Impulse 2 is not just a technical feat; it is a symbol of sustainable innovation, proving that ecological solutions can be found even in traditionally energy-hungry sectors such as aviation.

The success of Solar Impulse 2 has inspired other projects aimed at harnessing solar energy for a variety of applications, both in aviation and in other modes of transport. This historic flight ushers in a new era in which an aircraft's autonomy is no longer limited by the fuel on board, but by its ability to harness and use available natural resources.

# Fact 99 - First flight through an active volcano

In 1982, a British Airways commercial flight, Flight 9, unwittingly passed through a cloud of volcanic ash from the eruption of Mount Galunggung in Indonesia. This flight, carried out by a Boeing 747, made aviation history as the first to face such a situation, demonstrating just how much an aircraft can be tested by unpredictable natural forces.

The incident occurred while the aircraft was flying at an altitude of 37,000 feet. Without warning, the aircraft's four engines shut down after sucking in abrasive volcanic ash, causing a total loss of power. Passengers, and even the crew, were faced with an unprecedented emergency situation. The captain began an emergency descent, while trying to relight the engines, a critical maneuver that put the lives of everyone on board at stake.

Despite the gravity of the situation, the crew's composure enabled them to overcome the crisis. After a descent of over 20,000 feet, three engines were restarted, enabling the aircraft to stabilize its flight. Flight 9 finally landed safely in Jakarta, although the cabin was damaged by St. Elmo's lightning, a rare luminous phenomenon caused by static electricity in the ash.

This incident had a profound impact on civil aviation. It led to a better understanding of the dangers of volcanic ash for aircraft, prompting revisions to aviation safety protocols. Airlines and regulators have since developed more advanced detection systems and specific emergency procedures to deal with such events.

British Airways Flight 9 has gone down in history as a striking example of human and technological resilience. This flight, which went through one of the most dangerous situations in aviation, helped to improve flight safety worldwide, by raising awareness of the risks of extreme natural phenomena that aircraft can encounter.

# Fact 100 - The plane that survived the strongest turbulence

In 1966, a Braniff Airways Boeing 707 survived one of the most violent turbulences ever recorded, demonstrating the robustness of modern aircraft. The plane was flying over the Pacific Ocean when it was suddenly caught in unexpected turbulence, a weather phenomenon dreaded by pilots. The extreme turbulence shook the aircraft with such force that several passengers and crew were thrown against the cabin ceiling.

The severity of the turbulence was such that the Boeing 707 suffered significant structural damage, including deformation of the wings. The flight, which had started under normal flying conditions, ended up in total chaos, defying the limits of what commercial aircraft were expected to withstand at the time. The pilot, with remarkable composure, managed to stabilize the aircraft despite the incessant shaking.

After weathering the storm, the plane was able to resume flight, albeit with serious damage. The success of this feat was due not only to the pilot's experience, but also to the robust design of the Boeing 707, an aircraft model known for its solidity. The passengers, although shaken and some slightly injured, all survived the incident.

This event marked a turning point in the study of air turbulence. It prompted engineers to review designs to further strengthen aircraft structures in the face of these unpredictable forces. It also made airlines and regulators aware of the importance of training pilots to handle these extreme situations.

The Braniff Airways Boeing 707 incident remains a testament to the ability of aircraft to survive extreme conditions, reinforcing confidence in the safety of commercial aviation even in the face of the unexpected. This event has left a lasting imprint on aviation history, reminding us that, despite technological advances, the skies retain a degree of unpredictability.

# Conclusion

You've just been through a hundred facts that illustrate the incredible epic of aviation. As you've flown over these milestones, you've discovered how man pushed back the limits of what was possible, daring to defy gravity to conquer the skies. Aviation is not just a series of technical feats, it's also a human adventure that tells the story of our ceaseless quest for freedom and innovation.

These facts have shown you that aviation is much more than just a method of transport. It's a discipline that has transformed the way we see the world, shortening distances, bringing cultures closer together, and opening up horizons that were once inaccessible. Every innovation, every challenge overcome, bears witness to the determination and creativity of those who have shaped the history of flight.

You've explored moments of triumph and discovery, but also of challenge and danger. Aviation is a story of courage, perseverance, and a fierce will to overcome the unknown. These stories show that flying has never been an easy task, but a constant ambition to rise above earthly limits.

As you close this book, I hope you've found not only fascinating facts, but also a source of inspiration. The history of aviation is a reminder that innovation knows no boundaries, and that the boldest dreams can become reality with enough passion and determination. The sky, once distant and inaccessible, is now a frontier we cross every day.

Thank you for sharing this journey through aviation history. May these facts remind you that daring and ingenuity can take us far beyond our aspirations, and that, as aviation has proven, even the sky is no limit. May your spirit continue to fly high, inspired by the wonders you've discovered here.

*Marc Dresqui*

# Quiz

**1) What was the name of the first solar-powered plane to cross the English Channel in 1981?**

    a)    Solar Impulse
    b)    Sun Flyer
    c)    Solar Challenger
    d)    Helios

**2) What was the name of the first airplane to be marketed as a do-it-yourself kit?**

    a)    Piper Cub
    b)    Cessna 150
    c)    Bowers Fly Baby
    d)    Vans RV-4

**3) Which explorer made the first flight around the North Pole in 1926?**

    a)    Roald Amundsen
    b)    Charles Lindbergh
    c)    Richard E. Byrd
    d)    Amelia Earhart

**4) What is the fastest unmanned aircraft ever built, reaching a record speed of Mach 9.6 in 2004?**

    a)    Lockheed SR-71 Blackbird
    b)    North American X-15
    c)    North American X-43A
    d)    Boeing X-37

**5) Which aircraft made the first successful single-engine flight in 1903?**

    a)    Blériot XI
    b)    Wright Flyer
    c)    Curtiss Jenny
    d)    Sopwith Camel

**6) Which World War I aircraft was equipped with an open cockpit and became one of the most feared fighters of its time?**

    a)    Fokker Dr.I
    b)    Spad S.XIII
    c)    Sopwith Camel
    d)    Albatros D.III

**7) What is the widest aircraft ever built, with a wingspan of 117 metres, designed to launch rockets carrying satellites into orbit?**

    a)   Airbus A380
    b)   Hughes H-4 Hercules
    c)   Stratolaunch
    d)   Antonov An-225

**8) Which commercial aircraft was capable of flying at Mach 2, twice the speed of sound?**

    a)   Boeing 747
    b)   Lockheed SR-71 Blackbird
    c)   Concorde
    d)   Airbus A340

**9) Which aviator made the first aircraft take-off from an aircraft carrier in 1910?**

    a)   Charles Lindbergh
    b)   Howard Hughes
    c)   Eugene Ely
    d)   Orville Wright

**10) Which aircraft is designed to withstand storms and penetrate the heart of hurricanes to collect meteorological data?**

    a)   Boeing 747
    b)   Lockheed WC-130 Hercules
    c)   Douglas DC-3
    d)   F-22 Raptor

**11) At which event did Jimmy Doolittle perform a very low-level flight over a lake, demonstrating his exceptional piloting skills?**

    a)   The Gordon Bennett Cup
    b)   The Paris Air Show
    c)   The Schneider Trophy
    d)   The 1932 Olympic Games

**12) Which plane was the first to cross the equator on a round-the-world flight in 1924?**

    a)   Spirit of St. Louis
    b)   The Flyer
    c)   Douglas World Cruiser "Chicago
    d)   The Vin Fiz

**13) Which aircraft is specially designed for rescue missions, capable of operating in hostile environments and transporting casualties?**

    a)   Boeing 747

b) Lockheed C-130 Hercules
c) Concorde
d) Airbus A380

## 14) Which World War II aircraft, nicknamed "The Wooden Wonder", was built entirely of wood?

a) Spitfire
b) P-51 Mustang
c) De Havilland Mosquito
d) B-17 Flying Fortress

## 15) Which aircraft has the longest fuselage in the world?

a) Airbus A380
b) Boeing 777-300ER
c) Boeing 747-8
d) Airbus A350-1000

## 16) Which aircraft holds the record for the highest altitude reached?

a) SR-71 Blackbird
b) Boeing 747
c) Lockheed U-2
d) Concorde

## 17) In what year was the first flight made up entirely of blind passengers?

a) 1929
b) 1935
c) 1932
d) 1940

## 18) Which aircraft holds the record for the longest flight range?

a) Airbus A380
b) Boeing 747-8
c) Boeing 777-200LR
d) Concorde

## 19) Which aircraft was the first to fly with a nuclear reactor on board?

a) Boeing B-52 Stratofortress
b) Convair NB-36H
c) Lockheed SR-71 Blackbird
d) Northrop Grumman B-2 Spirit

## 20) What type of aircraft survived one of the most violent turbulences ever recorded in 1966?

a) Douglas DC-8
b) Lockheed L-1011 TriStar

c) Boeing 707
d) Airbus A300

# Answers

**1) What was the name of the first solar-powered plane to cross the English Channel in 1981?**

Correct answer: c) Solar Challenger

**2) What was the name of the first airplane to be marketed as a do-it-yourself kit?**

Correct answer: c) Bowers Fly Baby

**3) Which explorer made the first flight around the North Pole in 1926?**

Correct answer: c) Richard E. Byrd

**4) What is the fastest unmanned aircraft ever built, reaching a record speed of Mach 9.6 in 2004?**

Correct answer: c) North American X-43A

**5) Which aircraft made the first successful single-engine flight in 1903?**

Correct answer: b) Wright Flyer

**6) Which World War I aircraft was equipped with an open cockpit and became one of the most feared fighters of its time?**

Correct answer: c) Sopwith Camel

**7) What is the widest aircraft ever built, with a 117-metre wingspan, designed to launch rockets carrying satellites into orbit?**

Correct answer: c) Stratolaunch

**8) Which commercial aircraft was capable of flying at Mach 2, twice the speed of sound?**

Correct answer: c) Concorde

**9) Which aviator made the first aircraft take-off from an aircraft carrier in 1910?**

Correct answer: c) Eugene Ely

**10) Which aircraft is designed to withstand storms and penetrate the heart of hurricanes to collect meteorological data?**

Correct answer: b) Lockheed WC-130 Hercules

**11) At which event did Jimmy Doolittle perform a very low-level flight over a lake, demonstrating his exceptional piloting skills?**

Correct answer: c) Schneider Trophy

**12) Which plane was the first to cross the equator on a round-the-world flight in 1924?**

Correct answer: c) Douglas World Cruiser "Chicago

**13) Which aircraft is specially designed for rescue missions, capable of operating in hostile environments and transporting casualties?**

Correct answer: b) Lockheed C-130 Hercules

**14) Which World War II aircraft, nicknamed "The Wooden Wonder", was built entirely of wood?**

Correct answer: c) De Havilland Mosquito

**15) Which aircraft has the longest fuselage in the world?**

Correct answer: c) Boeing 747-8

**16) Which aircraft holds the record for the highest altitude reached?**

Correct answer: c) Lockheed U-2

**17) In what year was the first flight made up entirely of blind passengers?**

Correct answer: c) 1932

**18) Which aircraft holds the record for the longest flight range?**

Correct answer: c) Boeing 777-200LR

**19) Which aircraft was the first to fly with a nuclear reactor on board?**

Correct answer: b) Convair NB-36H

**20) What type of aircraft survived one of the most violent turbulences ever recorded in 1966?**

Correct answer: c) Boeing 707

Made in United States
Orlando, FL
19 December 2024

56181698R00068